202
WAYS NOT TO
MOOCH OFF
YOUR PARENTS

DATE DUE

SEP 1 2 2007	

Other titles by James Stephenson

- *202 Things to Make and Sell for Big Profits*

- *202 Things You Can Buy and Sell for Big Profits*

- *202 Services You Can Sell for Big Profits*

- *202 Ways to Supplement Your Retirement Income*

- *Ultimate Homebased Business Handbook: How to Start, Run, and Grow Your Own Profitable Business*

- *Ultimate Small Business Marketing Guide: 1,500 Great Marketing Tricks That Will Drive Your Business Through the Roof*

- *Ultimate Start-Up Directory*

202

WAYS NOT TO MOOCH OFF YOUR PARENTS

JAMES STEPHENSON

Ep
Entrepreneur®
Press

Editorial director: Jere L. Calmes
Cover design: Beth Hansen-Winter
Composition and production: Eliot House Productions

This publication is designed to provide accurate and authoritative information in regard to the
subject matter covered. It is sold with the understanding that the publisher is not engaged in ren-
dering legal, accounting, or other professional services. If legal advice or other expert assistance is
required, the services of a competent professional person should be sought.

Library of Congress Cataloging-in-Publication Data
Stephenson, James, 1966–.
    202 ways not to mooch off your parents/by James Stephenson.
      p.   cm.
    ISBN 1-932531-93-9 (alk. paper)
    1. Money-making projects for children—Juvenile literature. 2. Entrepreneurship—Juvenile
literature. 3. Small business—Juvenile literature. I. Title: Two hundred and two ways not to
mooch off your parents. II. Title.
HF5392.S74 2006
650.1'2083—dc22   2005028629

Printed in Canada

CONTENTS

CHAPTER 5

Making and Selling Simple Products _ _ _ _ _ _ _ _ _ _ 57

CHAPTER 6

Sports and Recreational Opportunities _ _ _ _ _ _ _ _ 73

CHAPTER 7

Online and Computer Businesses _____ 81

CHAPTER 8

Pet-Related Businesses _____ 89

PREFACE

My foray into business came early, at the tender age of 11; a friend and I decided to start a lawn mowing service, which happened quite literally by accident. We were scrounging around garage sales looking for a cheap lawn mower to buy so we could remove the wheels and use them on a go-cart we were building. We found a rusty old Lawn Boy that ran amazingly well. A few minutes of negotiations and it was ours for five bucks. I am not sure which one of us hatched the idea to start a lawn mowing service, but somewhere between the garage sale and my home, the schemed was cooked, and we were convinced we were on the road to riches. Armed with much enthusiasm and our old lawn mower we hit the road early the following morning, knocking on doors and offering our grass cutting services. Three doors later we had our first job, which we really messed up bad, leaving patches of long grass mixed with bare patches down to the dirt. In fact, we did such a lousy job that the homeowner lectured us for 20 minutes on the value of hard work and doing a good job. He reluctantly paid us $5, but told us our service would no longer be required.

That was the first and last job for my friend Jeff; the lecture scared him off and I guess that he figured collecting his allowance every week for doing zip was much easier than having to work for it. I was thrilled, $5 for 30 minutes work seemed like a fortune in 1978, not to mention that we had earned back our entire investment on only one job. I bought Jeff out and the lawn mower and business were officially mine. By the end of that summer, I learned the value of hard work and had become very good at cutting grass. Best of all, I was earning an average of $60 per week and some weeks more than $100. Almost 30 years later I am still self-employed and I still practice the lessons I learned from running the grass cutting service—provide quality and reliability at a fair price and you will succeed in business and earn a better than average income. It really is that simple.

My objective in creating this book was twofold: One, to identify the best ways that young people aged 12 to early 20s can earn extra money and two, to give them the information and tools that they need to know to get started in a simple-to-use step-by-step format. If you are in this age group, *202 Ways Not to Mooch Off Your Parents* is one of the few books you will find that is solely focused on what you can do to start making extra money right now. It is also the most up-to-date and resource-packed. The information and ideas featured in this book have been specifically developed to walk you through every step that is required to start and run a moneymaking enterprise for maximum success and profit.

If you are under the age of 18, your parents or legal guardian will have to act on your behalf on a number of legal and financial issues, including but not limited to, registering the business, preparing and signing legal documents, signing and executing contracts, preparing and filing tax and income forms and statements, and some financial matters such as opening bank accounts, merchant credit card accounts, and obtaining loans.

Getting Started with Making Extra Money

The question that every young person wants answered is, "How much extra money can I earn?" The answer is "it depends." It depends on which moneymaking enterprise you choose to start, the sales and marketing efforts you put forth, and how much time you can devote to it. That said, throughout this book you will find the information and tools you need to meet and exceed your income goals. You'll also find help determining what the right moneymaking venture is for you, taking into consideration issues such as doing something that you love, capitalizing on your current skills and knowledge, and the amount of money you have to invest to get started.

Getting started in any new moneymaking enterprise is always the hardest step, but you will learn all you need to know to get started in an easy-to-use, step-by-step format and how to earn a ton of extra cash once you get rolling.

Legal, Financial, and Safety Issues

When starting any moneymaking venture there are always legal, financial, and safety issues to consider, especially for younger entrepreneurs. To help demystify these issues you will learn everything that is required to start and operate a legal business including how to register a business name, select a legal business structure, and how to obtain required licenses and permits.

It also takes money to start a business or small moneymaking enterprise; you'll learn how to calculate how much money you will need, what funding sources are available to you, and how you can get started on a shoestring budget. You will learn money management issues such as how to set up simple bookkeeping practices, open a bank account, and some things you'll need to know about income tax and small business taxation.

Finally, since the world is not always a nice place, information has been included to make safety a top priority for every young entrepreneur and provide your parents with peace of mind knowing that all precaution have been taken in terms of health and safety issues.

Planning and Building Your Moneymaking Enterprise

Every new business or moneymaking enterprise, regardless of size, needs to be researched and planned so you can minimize financial risks while maximizing the potential for success and profitability. To establish a rock-solid foundation to build upon, you will find out how to develop a simple business plan that can be used as a roadmap to guide your new business and marketing strategies.

Depending on your venture, your business and marketing plans do not have to be highly sophisticated. Even a few well-researched and documented pages covering the basics are often sufficient to reveal the information you need to describe your business, identify your customers, reveal your product's or service's beneficial advantages, and develop marketing strategies. Inside you will learn how to put all this on paper.

Sales, Advertising, and Providing Great Customer Service

You will soon discover what you need to do to market and sell your products and services like a seasoned pro, and learn secrets that top young entrepreneurs and all successful business people use daily to sell more products and services for more profits. This book will also show you how to sell your products and services from home, in a retail environment, and even how to sell products wholesale or on consignment. And let's not forget about the internet, especially when e-commerce sales are expected to reach $230 billion by 2008! We'll show you how to start doing business online.

There are also a great number of excellent selling opportunities in every community—trade shows, consumer shows, flea markets, and craft fairs—and you'll learn what is needed to easily sell your products and services at these events for maximum profitability. You will learn amazing advertising secrets that will show you how to write attention-grabbing newspaper ads and create red-hot fliers to promote your products and services.

The Best 202 Ways to Earn Extra Money

Now the real fun begins. Chapters 5 through 17 are entirely devoted to informing you about the best 202 ways that you can earn extra money—selling products, providing services, manufacturing simple products, working with pets, or starting a food-related business, just to name a few. Each moneymaking opportunity includes a description of the venture, how to effectively market and sell, and helpful resources to take you to the next level. The resources featured include American and Canadian private corporations, business associations, government agencies, web sites, publications, products, services, and lots more.

All of the resources featured throughout were active web links, telephone numbers, and mailing addresses at the time of writing. Over time, however, some information changes or is no longer available. In an effort to ensure resource information remains beneficial and active for the long term, I have tried to include only reputable sources to feature as resources. That said, featuring a resource in this book is by no means an endorsement of the company, organization, product, or service. It is the responsibility of every young entrepreneur to do his or her own research to make sure they are doing business with reputable firms and individuals.

Resource icons used represent the following:

- ♂ A mouse icon represents an online resource web site address.
- ☎ A telephone icon represents a resource's contact telephone number.
- 📖 A book icon represents a book or other publication that offers further information.

■   ■   ■

202 Ways Not to Mooch Off Your Parents is the most authoritative and comprehensive book available on the topic. It gives you the ability to identify the best ways for *you* to earn extra money, as well as the information and tools you need to get started right now. Harness the power of this book by putting it to work for you today.

CHAPTER

GETTING STARTED

Every young person's dream is to have lots of extra cash, but if you did have lots of extra cash what would you use it for? I suppose many young people would say they would spend it—at the movies, on sporting activities, or to buy their first cars. There is nothing wrong with that. As the saying goes, you're only young once, so enjoy it while you can. But at the same time, you should also save a percentage of the money you earn and invest it in stocks, bonds, or a college education fund.

My advice would be to save at least 50 percent of the money you earn and use the rest for entertainment, sports, or hobby pursuits. A certain percentage of young people who start a business might also want to save the money they earn so that they can expand their businesses and not only continue operating them but turn them into full-time profitable enterprises after they have finished school. Consequently, even before you start earning extra money you'll want to carefully consider what the best use of that money is and develop a saving and investment strategy to maximize the future value of your hard work today.

Likewise, you also have to strike a balance in your personal life and remember that in addition to starting and operating a new business or moneymaking venture, you also have to keep up your educational studies and spend time with your family, participate in sports, other social activities, and just hang out with friends. In this chapter the various moneymaking options are discussed, as well as how much extra money you can earn, and what to consider when selecting a new business or moneymaking enterprise.

Moneymaking Options

This book is not about employment options for young people or how to land a job. It is about starting a business or moneymaking enterprise so that you can earn extra cash, or in some cases as much as a full-time income that would make most adults envious. With that goal in mind, options include providing services, selling products, or making and selling simple products, all of which are discussed below.

Provide a Service

The first option is to provide a service(s), such as dog walking, car washing, or grass cutting. The best thing about providing a service is that everyone is qualified regardless of age because we all have a skill, knowledge, or experience that other people are willing to pay for in the form of a service that you provide; or they are willing to pay you to teach them your specific skill or knowledge. Providing a service knows no boundaries—any young person with a need or desire to earn extra money can sell and provide a service. In later chapters you will find many services that you can provide to earn money, from window washing to errand running to computer training and lots of other moneymaking opportunities in between. Providing a service is a great option for young entrepreneurs because in many instances the initial investment to get started is little more than business cards and a bit of initial advertising, and often not even that. If selling services appeals to you, and you would like even more ideas than are featured throughout this book, then I would suggest that you pick up a copy of 📖 *202 Services You Can Sell for Big Profits* (Entrepreneur Press, 2005). It isn't specifically for young people, but there are still lots of ideas a young person could use.

Sell Products

Another possibility is to purchase new products, such as sunglasses, clothing, fashion accessories, furniture, or gifts in huge quantities and at wholesale prices and resell these items for a profit. You can sell them from home, online, at flea markets, from mall kiosks, or a vending cart in town. Or you might choose to purchase secondhand products, such as furniture, antiques, collectibles, cars, restaurant equipment, or books at bargain basement prices by scouring garage sales, flea markets, business closeouts, auction sales, and classified ads, and resell these items for a profit using many of the same venues from which you purchased them. Like providing a service, selling new or used products knows no boundaries, and everyone is qualified regardless of age and experience. If buying and selling new and used products appeals to you, and you would like even more ideas than are featured throughout this book, then I would suggest that you pick up a copy of 📖 *202 Things You Can Buy and Sell for Big Profits* (Entrepreneur Press, 2004)

Manufacture Simple Products

A third option is to manufacture and sell a product(s) at retail prices directly to consumers, or at wholesale prices and in bulk directly to other businesses such as retailers, exporters, wholesalers, and distributors. I know that I am starting to sound like a broken record, but once again, everyone is qualified because we all know how to make something, or with basic training can quickly learn how to make a simple product that can be sold for a profit. Ideally, you will want to start with something you already know and turn a hobby such as making stuff from wood or quilting into a profitable business venture. However, there are also literally hundreds of products that can easily be made at home with just basic training, and then sold for big profits. Just a few of these include candles, soap, toys, clothing, art, jewelry, furniture, garden products, herbs, birdhouses, and picture frames. If manufacturing and selling simple products appeals to you, and you would like even more ideas than are featured throughout this book, then I would suggest that you pick up a copy of 📖 *202 Things You Can Make and Sell for Big Profits* (Entrepreneur Press, 2005).

How Much Money Can You Earn?

How much extra money do you want to earn? I have to put the answer in the form of a question because operating your own business, even if it is a small part-time moneymaking enterprise, almost always gives you the potential to earn more money than you would be able to by working a job. Why? One reason is simple duplication. When you work for someone else, there is only you and only so many hours in the day to work for a specific set wage. When you operate a business, you can duplicate yourself by hiring employees and therefore increase productivity and duplicate your customers; if you are really ambitious you can even duplicate your business by opening in new geographical areas to sell more products and services to more customers and earn more profits and income. Without question, there are upper limits to how much money you can earn operating a small business, but at the same time your ability to earn an above-average income or a ton of extra cash will be determined by your ambition and motivation, and not by punching a time clock trading hours for a wage.

Another topic worth discussing in terms of earning income and profits is that the internet also gives young entrepreneurs access to a global audience of buying consumers. The internet makes it easier for small business owners to market and sell products and services into the global marketplace using online sales venues such as eBay, internet malls, affiliate programs, and e-storefronts, as well as your own web site. Now with the simple click of a mouse you can promote and sell your products and services to consumers worldwide, offering the opportunity to make more sales and earn more income and profits. As e-commerce continues to expand, it provides all entrepreneurs an excellent opportunity to earn extra income selling products and services online.

Choosing the Right Moneymaking Opportunity

The type of business or moneymaking opportunity that you are considering must suit you. You may have an interest and even experience in a specific business, selling a product, providing a specific service, or making and selling a product, but that does not necessarily make it a good thing for you to do to make money. There are many points to consider when finding a good match, including doing what you want and believe that you would enjoy, capitalizing on current skills and experiences, the amount of money you have to invest to get started, and if you are younger than 16 or so, obtaining parental permission and support. All of these topics are discussed in this chapter, and many of these topics are also discussed in greater detail throughout the book.

Do What You Love

I cannot stress enough that you should do what you love to do to earn extra money, or at least something that you believe that you will enjoy. If you do not like what you are doing, chances are you won't stick with it for long, and even if you do, you probably won't be motivated to do a good job. What you get out of your business or moneymaking opportunity in the form of satisfaction, money, and enjoyment will be the direct result of what you put into your business. If you do not enjoy what you are doing, it is safe to assume that will be reflected in the success (or lack of it) of your business. All successful businesspeople, regardless of their ages, share a common trait: They love what they do. If you enjoy fitness, consider starting a personal trainer service; if you like the great outdoors, then seek out an opportunity that will get you working outside; or if you love animals, then start a pet sitting business, dog walking service, or any other number of opportunities that will enable you to work with animals. The old saying "Do what you love and the money will follow" is great advice. Ultimately, if you do not think that you would enjoy it, then don't start. You can't stay motivated and rise to new challenges if you do not like what you're doing.

Capitalize on Your Skills and Knowledge

The first thing you should know about capitalizing on your skills and knowledge is not to worry if you lack business skills and experience in areas such as selling and bookkeeping. These are important skills to have, but at the same time they are also all skills that you can learn. More important is the question, "What specific skill or specialized knowledge do you currently have that can be used to start your own business or moneymaking opportunity?" Skills and knowledge that you possess are your best, and by far your most marketable asset. For instance, if you know how to pay the piano, that is a skill that other people will pay you to teach them. Or, if you know how to build a birdhouse, that is also a skill that you can capitalize on by starting your own birdhouse manufacturing and sales business.

Every young person has one or more skills that other people are prepared to pay for in the form of a service provided to them or a product they need and want. However, with that said, most people have a tendency to underestimate the true value of their skills, experiences, and knowledge. But keep this in mind: What may come naturally to you may not come so naturally to others. Likewise, you might think that your particular knowledge or expertise may be of little value, but if someone else needs or wants to learn about that knowledge, needs the service, or needs the product, it is very valuable to them. Create a list of all of your skills, experiences, and specific knowledge. Then look for ways to build a business or moneymaking opportunity around one or more of these.

Start-Up Funding

Another important issue you need to consider in terms of finding a good match is the amount of money that you have to start a business. The first question to answer is, do you have, or have access to the money needed to start the business? If not, it is probably not a good match (at least right now), and you should consider alternatives. An alternative might be to start a different type of business that requires less money to get rolling, or find a partner to help share the costs of the business start-up and workload. The money needed to start a business (called "investment capital") can be broken into two categories: The first is start-up capital—what you need to purchase equipment, meet legal requirements, or buy inventory, for example. The second is working capital—the money you need to pay all the bills until the business is earning money and reaches a break-even point. Unfortunately, more times than not, a new business that is started without enough money will ultimately fail. This is the harsh reality of the business world. On a positive note, the vast majority of young people who start a business have little in the way of personal expenses to pay (such as rent or mortgage payments), which means that you can use most of your start-up money for the business, not needing it to cover personal bills, giving the business a better chance for success. Likewise, many of the opportunities featured in this book can be started for less than a few thousand dollars, and lots for as little as $100. Therefore, while having or having access to enough start-up funding and working capital is important, if you don't, you will still be able to find a moneymaking opportunity in this book that is right for you.

Parental Permission and Support

A good match also means that you have full parental permission and support to start and operate a business or moneymaking enterprise. Parental permission is an important one, because if you are underage, your parents or legal guardian will need to act on your behalf and sign or cosign any number of legal, financial, and insurance documents depending on what business you choose.

Equally important is parental support, because in many instances you will be relying on your parents or other family members to help out with your venture. This could mean borrowing the family car, having parents drive you around for various business-related reasons, or using space in the family home to store things or set up an office or work area, just to mention a few. Therefore you should discuss your business desires and plans with your parents to get their full permission and support for your venture before making any decisions.

CHAPTER

LEGAL, FINANCIAL, AND SAFETY ISSUES

When starting any business or moneymaking enterprise there are always legal, financial, and safety issues to consider, such as registering a business name, selecting a legal business structure, obtaining a business license and sales tax ID number, shopping for insurance coverage, opening a commercial bank account, and preparing and filing business and income tax returns. This chapter will help demystify these issues and give you the information and tools you need to establish and operate a legal, financially sound, and safe enterprise.

7

Starting a Legal Business

Do you need to make your business or moneymaking enterprise "legal"? The short answer is yes, but the long answer is that it greatly depends on what you plan on doing to earn extra money. For instance, if you plan on selling products at flea markets, online, or in other retail environments then the answer is yes. However, if you plan on shoveling snow, cutting grass, and raking leaves around the neighborhood to earn a few extra bucks, you do not need to worry about going through all the steps unless you employ people and expand the business to the point of considerable sales. Then Uncle Sam will want a share of the profits.

The starting point is to choose and register a business name and to select a legal business structure, which can be a sole proprietorship, a partnership, a corporation, or a limited liability corporation, all of which are discussed below.

Under-18 Business Law

Long before you start to think about starting a legal business you should know that young people under the age of 18 in both the United States and Canada are prohibited from forming a legal business entity. What this means is that if you want to form a legal business you must get your parents or legal guardian to do so on your behalf. This is true for a number of legal issues, including but not limited to registering the business, preparing and signing legal documents, signing and executing contracts, preparing and filing tax and income forms and statements, and taking charge of financial matters such as opening bank accounts and merchant credit card accounts, and obtaining loans.

Registering a Business Name

If you start a legal business, and regardless of the legal structure you choose, you need to select and register a business name. You can name the business after your name, such as Cindy's Mobile Dog Wash, or you can choose a fictitious business name, such as On-Time Mobile Dog Wash. It is important to remember that your business name will promote your business and get used regularly in print and conversation (all known as "marketing"). Therefore, your business name should be descriptive enough to be an effective marketing tool—so that when you say your business name, people know what you do. It should also be short, easy to spell, easy to pronounce, and very memorable. You have to think of visual impact and word-of-mouth referrals; both of these rely on short, easy-to-spell-and-remember, descriptive names.

Business name registration costs vary by state and province, but generally, it costs less than $200 to register a sole proprietorship, including name search fees.

In the United States, you can register your business name through the Small Business Administration (SBA). Log on to ♂ www.sba.org to find an office near you. In Canada you can register your business through a provincial Canadian Business Service Center. Log on to ♂ www.cbsc.org to find an office near you.

Sole Proprietorship and Partnerships

The most common, and basic, legal business structures are a sole proprietorship and a partnership. A sole proprietorship means that you are the sole owner of the business. It is the simplest and least expensive type of business structure to start and maintain. A sole proprietorship means your business entity and your personal affairs are all as one—a single tax return, personal liability for all business debts and actions, and control of all revenues and profits. Outside of routine business registrations, permits, and licenses, there are few government regulations on sole propreitorships.

If you and a friend or family member decide to start a business together, then a partnership is a good legal structure. A partnership allows two or more people to start, operate, and own a business. Make sure the partnership is based on a written agreement, not just a verbal agreement. The agreement should cover issues such as financial investment, income and profit distribution, duties of each partner, and exit strategy should one partner want out of the agreement. Business profits are split among partners proportionate to their ownership (for instance, if you "own" 60 percent of the business, you get 60 percent of the profits and your partner gets 40 percent) and are treated as taxable personal income. Perhaps the biggest advantage of a partnership is that both financial risk and work are shared by more than one person. This enables each partner to specialize within the business for the benefit of the collective business team.

In the United States, you can register a sole proprietorship or partnership through the Small Business Administration (SBA). Log on to ♂ www.sba.org to find an office near you. In Canada you can register through a provincial Canadian Business Service Center. Log on to ♂ www.cbsc.org to find an office near you.

Corporation and Limited Liability Corporation

Two more legal business structure options include a corporation and a limited liability corporation (LLC). The most complicated business structure is the corporation. When you form a corporation, you create a legal entity that is separate and distinct from the shareholders of the corporation. Because the corporation becomes its own entity, "it" pays taxes, assumes debt, can legally sue, can be legally sued, and, as a tax-paying entity, must pay taxes on its taxable income (profit) prior to paying any dividends to the shareholders. But the company's finances and financial records are completely separate from those of the shareholders. The biggest advantage to incorporating your business is that you can greatly reduce your own personal liability if the company is sued or goes broke.

Like a corporation, a limited liability corporation provides protection from personal liabilities, but the tax advantages are those of a partnership. Limited liability corporations can be formed by one or more people, called LLC members, who alone or together organize a legal entity separate and distinct from the owners' personal affairs in most respects. The advantages of a limited liability corporation over a corporation or partnership are that it is less expensive to form and maintain than a corporation, offers protection from personal liability that partnerships do not provide, and has simplified taxation and reporting rules in comparison to a corporation. Because of these advantages, limited liability corporations have become the fastest-growing form of legal business structure in the United States.

In the United States, you can file a corporation or limited liability corporation online using a service such as The Corporation Company, ☌ www.corporate.com, or contact the American Bar Association, ☎ (202) 662-1000, ☌ www.abanet.org, to find a lawyer who specializes in corporate filing in your area. In Canada, you can file a corporation online using a service such as Canadian Corp, ☌ www.canadian corp.com, or contact the Canadian Bar Association, ☎ (800) 267-8860, ☌ www .cba.org, to find a lawyer who specializes in corporate filing in your area.

Business License and Permits

To legally operate a business in all municipalities in the United States and Canada, you will need to obtain a business license. Business license costs vary from $50 up to $1,000 per year, depending on your geographic location, expected sales, the type of business you are engaged in, and the types of services and products you sell. Business license costs vary from $50 up to $1,000 per year, depending on your geographic location, expected sales, the type of business you are engaged in, and the types of services and products you sell. Because they are issued at the municipal level, contact your city/county clerk's or permits office for the full requirements for a business license. The Small Business Administration (SBA) also provides an online directory indexed by state, outlining where business licenses can be obtained (☌ www.sba.gov/hotlist/license.html). In the United States and Canada, you can also contact the chamber of commerce to inquire about business license requirements and fees. Contact the chamber in the United States, ☌ www .chamber.com, and in Canada, ☌ www.chamber.ca.

Depending on the types of products and services you sell, there are various permits that you will also need to obtain, such as resale certificate, sales tax permit, ID number—but whatever you want to call them, you need a permit to collect and remit sales tax if you will be selling any products and even some services. Almost all states and provinces now impose a sales tax on products sold directly to consumers, or end users. It is the business owner's responsibility to collect and remit sales taxes. The same sales tax permits are needed when purchasing goods for resale from manufacturers and wholesalers so the goods can be bought tax-free. The SBA provides a directory indexed by state outlining where and how sales tax permits and ID numbers can be obtained, including information on completing and remitting sales tax forms. This directory is located at ♂ www.sba.gov/hotlist/license.html.

In Canada, there are two levels of sales tax, one charged by most provinces on the retail sale of products to consumers, and the second charged by the federal government. The second is known as the goods and services tax and is charged on the retail sale of all goods and most services. You can obtain a federal Goods and Services Sales/Harmonized Sales Tax (GST/HST) number by contacting the Canada Customs and Revenue Agency at ♂ www.ccra-adrc.gc.ca.

There are other licenses, permits, certificates, and laws that you may need to comply with in terms of starting and operating your business or selling certain products and services. These might include fire safety inspection permits, hazardous materials handling permits, import/export certificates, police clearance certificates, environmental laws, and laws pertaining to food and drug safety administered through the U.S. Food and Drug Administration (FDA). Keep in mind that the obligation is on the business owner to find out the laws and regulations that must be followed and the relevant permits and registrations that are required depending on the kind of busiess you start.

Insurance Coverage

Insurance protection is another important issue that young entrepreneurs have to consider when starting and operating a business enterprise. Again, if you operate a simple business, in most cases, insurance coverage of any sort will not be needed. However, if you are operating a more complicated venture, purchasing appropriate insurance is the only way that you can be 100 percent sure that in the event of a catastrophic event, your business, assets, and clients will be protected. Discussed in this section are a few of the more important types of insurance coverage, which include property, liability, and workers' compensation. Contact a licensed insurance agent or broker to help decipher insurance legalese for you and to find the best coverage for your needs at the lowest cost. In the United States, you can contact the Independent Insurance Agents and Brokers of America at ♂ www.iiaa.org. In Canada, you can contact the Insurance Brokers Association of Canada at ♂ www.ibac.ca.

Property Insurance

Some young entrepreneurs may operate their business ventures from their own rented residential locations or rented commercial spaces. But the vast majority will substantially manage or operate their business or moneymaking opportunities from their parents' homes. Depending on the type of business you start, you may or may not need separate property insurance, or to increase or alter the type of property insurance that is currently in force where the business will operate from. Property insurance generally covers buildings and structures on the property as well as the contents of those buildings. Most property insurance policies provide protection in the form of a cash settlement or paid repairs in the event of fire, theft, vandalism, flood, earthquake, wind damage, referred to as "acts of God." Floods and earthquakes generally require an addition to the policy known as a "rider." Property insurance is the starting point and can branch out to include separate coverage for specialized tools and equipment, office improvements, inventory, and various liability riders, if required.

As a rule of thumb, property insurance should protect buildings, property, improvements, tools, equipment, furniture, cash on hand, and accounts receivable and payable, as well as restricted liability. Additionally, special riders will be needed to cover working at your clients' locations as well as tools and equipment in transit to work sites. All insurance companies provide free quotes, but it is wise to obtain at least three so you can compare costs, coverage, deductibles, and reliability. If you are going to run an enterprise from your parents' home, make sure to have mom or dad contact the current insurance agent and ask questions specific to the business you will be operating to determine the appropriate level and type of coverage that may be needed.

Liability Insurance

No matter how diligent you are in taking all necessary precautions to protect your customers and yourself by removing potential perils from your business and the products and services you sell, you could still be held legally responsible for events beyond your control. Product misuse, third-party damages, and service misunderstandings have all been grounds for successful litigation in the United

States and Canada. As the old saying goes, "It's better to be safe than sorry." The best way to protect yourself is to get liability insurance that specifically provides protection for the type of business you operate and the products and services you sell. Extended liability insurance is often referred to as general business liability or umbrella business liability and insures a business against accidents and injury that might occur at the business location, at clients' locations, or other perils related to the products and services sold. General liability insurance provides protection from the costs associated with successful litigation or claims against your business or you, and covers such things as medical expenses, recovery expenses, and property damage. Again, keep in mind if you are only operating a simple enterprise, such as grass mowing to earn a few extra dollars over the summer, liability insurance is not necessarily needed.

Workers' Compensation Insurance

In the United States and Canada, workers' compensation insurance is mandatory for all the people your business employs. Workers' compensation insurance protects employees injured on the job by providing short- or long-term financial benefits as well as covering medical and rehabilitation costs directly resulting from an on-the-job injury. If you have no employees and operate your business as a sole proprietorship or partnership, workers' compensation insurance is not mandatory, unless your business is incorporated, then officers and any employees must be covered. Rates are based on industry classification, which generally means the more dangerous the work, the higher your premiums will be. Likewise, the more claims for workers' compensation your business files, the higher your rates will go. Because workers' compensation classifications, forms, and guidelines can be confusing, I would advise you to visit the U.S. Department of Labor Office of Workers' Compensation Programs online at, ♂ www.dol.gov/esa/owcp-org .htm. This web page has links to all states and the District of Columbia, explaining workers' compensation rules and regulations. In Canada, log on to ♂ www .awcbc.org, the Association of Workers' Compensation Boards of Canada, which provides links to all provincial and territorial compensation offices.

Financing Your New Business Venture

How much money do you need to start your new moneymaking enterprise? The answer depends on the type of business you plan to start, the products and services you will sell, equipment requirements, transportation needs, marketing, and many other things. Depending on your venture, you might only need $50 or as much as $25,000 to get started. In Chapter 3 you will find a handy start-up costs worksheet that can be used to help you determine how much money is needed.

The next question is, once you know how much money you will need, where will you get the money if you don't already have it? Options include using your own savings, borrowing from family or friends, or securing a government small business loan. All of these options are discussed below.

Once again, as you read through the information in this section, remember that if you are under the age of 18, your parents or legal guardian will have to act on your behalf on a number of legal and financial issues.

Personal Savings

The first way to finance your business enterprise or moneymaking venture is by using your own savings if funds are available. Self-funding is a good idea for most young entrepreneurs for a few reasons. One, in most cases the initial investment needed to get started is generally very low. Two, self-funding enables you to stay in control of how, when, and why money is spent and you will not feel anxious about whether or not you can get the proper funding, have to worry about debt accumulation, and there is no bank or investor loan and interest repayment to make each month.

"Love Loans"

Another way to fund a business start-up is to ask parents, siblings, extended family members, or friends for a loan. These loans are often referred to as "love loans." Of course, there is a potential downside to this: If your business venture were to fail, would you still be able to pay back the loan? If not, your relationship with the family member or friend who provided the loan could be damaged. But with that said, many successful business ventures have been started with "love loans" and flourished. If you decide to borrow from friends or family to fund your business, treat the transaction as you would if you were borrowing from a bank. Have a promissory note drawn up and signed (see Figure 2.1), noting the details of the agreement, and stick to it like glue.

Government Small Business Loans

In the United States and Canada, there are government programs in place to assist people starting a new business, and many of these programs are for young entrepreneurs. In the United States, these programs are administered through the Small Business Administration. In Canada, most small business financial aid and incentive programs are administered through the Business Development Bank of Canada. To

FIGURE 2.1: Sample Promissory Note

This loan agreement is by and between:

Borrower Information

Name _____

Address _____

City _____ State _____ Zip Code _____ Tel _____

Lender Information

Name _____

Address _____

City _____ State _____ Zip Code _____ Tel _____

I, (borrower's name here), promise to pay (lender's name here) the sum of $ _____, bearing interest at the rate of _____% per annum, and payable in _____ equal and consecutive monthly installments, commencing on the _____ day of each month until paid, with a final installment of $ _____ on the _____ day of _____, 20_____, upon which the loan shall be repaid in full with no further principal or interest amounts owing.

_____ _____   _____ _____
Borrower's Signature   Date   Lender's Signature   Date

_____ _____
Witnessed by   Date

learn about what government small business loan programs you might qualify for, contact the SBA or BDC through the contact information below.

United States
U.S. Small Business
   Administration (SBA)
Financial Programs
409 Third Street SW
Washington, DC 20416
☎ (800) 827-5722
✆ www.sba.gov/financing/

Canada
Business Development
   Canada
BDC Building
5 Place Ville Marie, Suite 400
Montreal, Quebec H3B 5E7
☎ (877) 232-2269
✆ www.bdc.ca

Money Management

Money management is an important skill for young entrepreneurs to learn and practice. Banking and keeping track of your money has to be a priority, even if you decide to hire an accountant or bookkeeper to look after the books. You will still need to familiarize yourself with basic bookkeeping and money management principles and activities such as understanding credit, reading bank statements and tax forms, and making sense of accounts receivable and accounts payable, especially if your enterprise is generating substantial sales. You also have to think about how you want your customers to pay—cash, checks, debit cards, credit cards, and online payment options, all of which are discussed below.

Opening a Business Bank Account

If your venture is small and your customers pay you in cash or by check made out in your name, a personal bank account is all you need. But if your venture is larger, and you accept credit cards, debit cards, business checks, and such you will need to open a business bank account. Setting up a business bank account is easy. Look for a bank that is small business friendly and call to arrange an appointment to open an account. When you go, make sure you take personal identity as well as your business name registration papers and business license because these are usually required to open a business bank account. Also keep in mind that if you are underage, you will need to take a parent or legal guardian along to sign the permission documents. Next, deposit some funds into your new account and order your new business checks; that is about it.

Bookkeeping

When it comes time to set up your financial books, you have two options—do it yourself (or enlist mom or dad to keep the books) or hire an accountant or book-keeper. You might want to do both by keeping your own books and hiring an accountant to prepare year-end financial statements and tax forms. If you opt to keep your own books, make sure you invest in accounting software such as QuickBooks, ♂ www.quickbooks.com, or Quicken, ♂ www.quicken.com, because they are easy to use. Most accounting programs also allow you to create invoices, track bank account balances and merchant account information, and keep track of accounts payable and receivable. If you are unsure about your bookkeeping abilities even with the aid of accounting software, you may wish to hire a bookkeeper to do your books on a monthly basis and a chartered accountant to audit the books quarterly and prepare year-end business statements and tax returns. If you are only washing windows a few days a month to earn a few extra dollars, there is little need for accounting software or accounting services. Simply invest in a basic ledger (available at all office supply stores) and record all business costs and sales to keep track of money coming in and money going out.

To find an accountant or bookkeeper in your area, you can contact the United States Association of Chartered Accountants, ☎ (212) 334-2078, 🖃 www.acaus.org, or the American Institute of Professional Bookkeepers, ☎ (800) 622-0121, 🖃 www.aipb.com. In Canada, you can contact the Chartered Accountants of Canada, ☎ (416) 977-3222 🖃 www.cica.ca, or the Canadian Bookkeepers Association, ☎ (604) 664-7576 🖃 www.c-b-a.ca.

Accepting Cash, Checks, and Debit Cards

Cash is the first way to get paid. Of course, the major downside is that cash is risky because you could get robbed or lose it. Even if you prefer not to receive cash, there are people who will pay in cash, so get in the habit of making bank deposits during daylight hours.

Checks are another popular payment method, especially for paying for services. Young entrepreneurs selling services will have to become comfortable with being paid with a personal check. Even so, you still have to take a few precautions to ensure you don't get left holding a rubber check. Ask to see picture ID and write the customer's driver's license number on the back. If the amount of the check exceeds a few hundred dollars, ask the buyer to get the check certified or pay with a bank draft instead. Also get in the habit of checking dates and dollar amounts to make sure they are correct and that your customer has signed the check.

The debit card is another option, but will require you to buy or rent a debit card terminal to accept debit card payments. Most banks and credit unions offer business clients debit card equipment and services. The processing equipment will set you back about $40 per month for a terminal connected to a conventional telephone line and about $100 per month for a cellular terminal, plus the cost of the telephone line or cellular service. There is also a transaction fee charged by the bank and payable by you every time there is a debit card transaction, which ranges from 10 cents to 50 cents per transaction, based on variables such as dollar value and frequency of use. Accepting payment by debit card is especially useful to young entrepreneurs selling products in a retail environment such as a flea market or mall kiosk.

Credit Card Merchant Account

Many consumers have replaced paper money all together in favor of plastic when buying products and services. So depending on the products or services that you sell, how these are sold, and expected sales volume, you might want to consider opening a credit card merchant account. This is especially true if you plan to do business on the web because credit cards and electronic cash transfers are used to complete almost all web sales and financial transactions. To establish a credit card merchant account, visit your bank or credit union, or contact a merchant account broker such as 1st American Card Service, ♂ www.1stamericancardservice.com, Cardservice International, ♂ www.cardservice.com, or Merchant Account Express, ♂ www.merchantexpress.com. Don't forget, if you are underage you will need a legal guardian to open the account.

The biggest advantage of opening a credit card merchant account is the fact that studies have proven that merchants who accept credit cards can increase sales by as much as 50 percent. This does come at a cost, especially when you consider you will have to pay an application fee, setup fee, purchase or rent processing equipment and software, pay administration and statement fees, and pay processing and transaction fees ranging from 2 to 8 percent on total sales volumes, but you can offset these fees by factoring them in when establishing retail selling prices and by increased sales.

Online Payment Services

Online payment services allow people and businesses to exchange currency electronically over the internet. These services are very popular with consumers and merchants. PayPal, ♂ www.paypal.com, is one of the more popular online payment services offering personal and business account services. Both types of accounts allow funds to be transferred electronically among members, but only the business account enables merchants to accept credit card payments for goods and services. Another popular online payment service is Veri Sign Pay Flow, ♂ www .verisign.com. Online payment services are quick, easy, and cheap to open, and you can receive payment from any customer with an e-mail account. You can also have the funds deposited directly into your account, have a check issued and mailed, or leave funds in your account to draw on using your debit card. If you plan on selling products or services online, offering customers online electronic payment options is a must.

Small Business Taxation

If you start and operate a legal business you will need to pay taxes on the money you earn, as well as the profits the business earns. Because small business taxation is complicated, you should seek professional help. The best information that you can obtain about small business and income taxation comes directly from the source, which is the Internal Revenue Service (IRS) in the United States, and Canada Customs and Revenue Agency (CCRA) in Canada.

The Internal Revenue Service provides a number of free publications that explain small business taxation issues that can be used as a guide for completing small business and self-employed tax forms. You can order IRS small business information, tax forms, and publications in person at your local IRS office, online at ☌ www.irs.gov, or toll-free for mail delivery by calling ☎ (800) 829-3676.

Canada Customs and Revenue Agency also provides a number of free publications that explain small business tax issues and can be used as a guide for completing small business tax and self-employed tax forms. You can order Canada Customs and Revenue Agency small business information, tax forms, and publications in person at your provincial business service centers, online at ☌ www.ccra-adrc.gc.ca/formspubs/request-e.html, or toll-free for mail delivery by calling ☎ (800) 959-2221.

Talking about Safety

In terms of safety, there are two important points to consider. One, not every person on this planet is a nice person. You must remain cautious when dealing with any adult, or any person for that matter, especially people that you do not know. Second, you must remember that your safety comes first. For instance, always make sure to follow safety precautions when using any equipment, such as wearing gloves, safety glasses, and safety boots when cutting grass, or having a second person to steady a ladder when using ladders for work.

In short, always make sure that you do not attempt an activity that could place you in a potentially dangerous situation. You have to know your limits and your surroundings at all times, and develop action and contingency plans to ensure that you remain safe, and that you have a plan to deal with worst-case scenarios. It is best to develop these plans with your parents. It is always a good idea, regardless of your age, to let people know where you are going, what you will be doing, how they can contact you, and when they can expect you back. Therefore, I would suggest that all young people should either have their own cell phones or be able to use family members' cell phones when away from home, regardless if it is for the day, or only for a few minutes.

3

PLANNING AND BUILDING YOUR MONEYMAKING ENTERPRISE

Think of planning and building your moneymaking enterprise as the point where the work begins—but the fun begins too. I say work because this is the point where you lay the foundation that your venture will be built upon, and fun because once complete, you will be one step closer to starting and earning money.

This chapter covers business and marketing planning, building a business team, developing a business image, taking your venture online, pricing products and services, and information about product packaging, delivery, and inventory management.

Business and Marketing Planning

In order to minimize financial risks while maximizing the potential for success and profitability, you need to research and plan your moneymaking enterprise. How sophisticated your business and marketing plans need to be depends on the business you choose. Even a few well-researched and documented pages covering the basics are often enough to describe your business, identify your customers, reveal your product's or service's beneficial advantages, and develop your marketing strategies. With that goal in mind, business plan information is broken into three areas—company information, marketing information, and financial information. Your business and marketing plan will act as a roadmap to lead you from business idea to success.

Company Information

The company section is where you describe your business in three subsections—business description, management team, and legal issues.

Business Description

In the business description area you want to provide a general overview of your business and the product(s) and services you sell. Include information such as the business name, location, and the legal structure—sole proprietorship, partnership, limited liability corporation, or corporation. Also note the business start date or expected start date, and briefly describe the current stage of your business's development.

Management Team

Next, you want to describe the management team, even if you are the sole owner and employee. The management team of any business consists of the key people running the business. Start by listing the owners of the business and describe their experience, training, and the duties each will perform. Then, list employees and describe their experience, training, remuneration, and the duties each will perform. Or if you plan on hiring employees in the future, describe what roles they will fill and the duties each will perform. Finally, list professional service providers (lawyers, consultants, accountants, etc.), and describe the services they will provide.

Legal Issues

Here you want to describe any legal issues in terms of setting up and operating your business, including legal issues that are specific to the products or services you intend on making, selling, or providing. Further, note all licenses, permits, or registrations that are needed, or that have been obtained, as well as the cost of each. A few of these might include business license, vendor permit, employer identification number, or sales tax permits. Also list your insurance requirements, such as general liability insurance, along with the cost and date each is needed to start. Finally, list and describe things known as intellectual properties—trademarks, patents, or copyrights that the business owns, has applied for, or will be using under license from the property owner. Include the nature of these intellectual properties, and the advantages associated with ownership or right of use.

Marketing Information

Marketing research and planning proves that there is sufficient demand for your product, and that you can compete in the marketplace. In the marketing section you want to describe your target customer, discuss competition, and cover the 4 Ps of marketing—product, price, place, and promotion. This information can then be used to guide your marketing decisions from where you are now to where you want to be in the future.

Target Customer Description

You have to know who the people are that are most likely to buy your product(s) or service(s): these are referred to as your "target customers." Researching, collecting, and recording this data enables you to create a target customer profile so you can aim your advertising, marketing, and sales activities directly at your target customers. This in turn saves you money and time by not targeting advertising and marketing activities that will be ineffective. What do you need to know about your target customers? You need to know:

- Where they are located geographically
- The percentage of male versus female
- Their age range, levels of education, marital status, and what they do to earn their livings
- What is most important to them when making purchasing decisions—price, value, service, warranty, or quality
- The publications they read, radio stations and programs they listen to, and television stations and programs they watch
- The types of recreational and social activities they participate in

Competition Description

You also need to know which other businesses are selling the same or similar products or services as you, in the same area, and to the same target customer known as your competition. You can use the information you gather and record about your competition to develop strategies to turn their weaknesses into your strengths, as well as capitalize on marketplace opportunities. Get started by listing your main competitors, describing their strengths and weaknesses, as well as what they do well that you should also be doing.

Also describe what strengths and resources your business has and how your products or services will be positioned in the marketplace—low price leader, quality above all, cater to the high-end segment of the market—in relation to your competitors.

Four Ps of Marketing

Developing your marketing strategy revolves around the four marketing Ps—product, price, place (distribution), and promotion. It is the combination of the four Ps that creates your marketing mix. Essentially, the four Ps are about finding the right combination of each, enabling you to create the perfect marketing mix comprised of the marketing strategies that will allow you to meet and exceed your marketing objectives.

- *Product.* Describe in detail the product(s) you make or sell, or the service(s) you provide including special features, how customers benefit from using the product or service, competitive advantages, guarantees, and any key research and development programs planned.
- *Price.* Describe how much you will charge, how you arrive at your selling price, and your pricing strategy. Also list competitor's prices, and how your customers can pay for their purchases, such as credit cards, debit cards, electronic transfers, as well as the benefits to your business and costs associated with providing these payment options.
- *Place (Distribution).* Describe the primary method you will utilize to sell your product or service (homebased, retail location, or wholesale), as well as secondary methods (eBay, trade shows, flea markets, consignment, craft shows, or other special events). Describe the operations system you will utilize to manage sales from initial order to delivery to after-sales customer service and follow-up.
- *Promotion.* Describe how you will advertise and promote your products and services—newspaper, online, and signs, as well as marketing materials such as fliers. Also detail any direct sales tactics you will employ, including personal contact selling, mail, telephone, and electronic.

Financial Information

Most young people feel intimidated by financial planning because of a lack of experience, but remember it only has to be as simple or as difficult as you want to make it. For a small venture you only have to cover the basics—funding requirements and funding sources. For larger ventures, there is additional financial data that should be included in business planning, things such as a breakeven analysis, balance sheet, income projections, and capital equipment and inventory lists. Business plan and accounting software programs such as Palo Alto, ♂ www.palo alto.com and QuickBooks, ♂ www.quickbooks.com, include customizable templates for financial forecasting and statements.

Funding Requirements

Describe how much money is needed to start your enterprise, what the money will be used for, and any future funding requirements. Start by describing your current funding requirements—purchasing tools, equipment, and inventory, and obtaining business permits, for example. Next, describe any future funding requirements and what the money will be used for—equipment upgrades or to develop a web site, for example. Equipment and inventory lists should include what you currently have, what is needed in the short term (less than 12 months), and what is needed for the long term (more than 12 months). Additionally, you should include the number of units required, the cost of each, and the date when the required items will be purchased.

Funding Sources

The next step is to identify and describe where the money will come from to meet your funding requirements—you, mom and dad, bank loan, or other family member—and how and when the money will be repaid if it is borrowed. If you are going to obtain money from more than one source, describe each. If this includes borrowing money to start your business or meet any funding need, describe the terms and conditions, including interest rate, and how the money will be repaid, including the repayment schedule.

Start-Up Costs Worksheet

Use the handy start-up costs worksheet (see Figure 3.1) to calculate how much money you will need to start your new business. Ignore items not relevant to your specific business start-up or moneymaking venture, and add items as required.

FIGURE 3.1: Start-Up Costs Worksheet

A. Business Setup

Business registration	$ _____
Business license	$ _____
Vendor permits	$ _____
Other permits	$ _____
Insurance	$ _____
Professional fees	$ _____
Training and education	$ _____
Bank account	$ _____
Merchant accounts	$ _____
Payment processing equipment	$ _____
Association fees	$ _____
Deposits	$ _____
Other _____	$ _____
Subtotal A	$ _____

B. Business Identity

Business cards	$ _____
Logo design	$ _____
Letterhead	$ _____
Envelopes	$ _____
Other _____	$ _____
Subtotal B	$ _____

C. Office/Storefront/Workshop

Rent deposit	$ _____
Damage deposit	$ _____
Communication equipment/devices	$ _____
Computer hardware	$ _____
Software	$ _____
Furniture	$ _____
Other office equipment	$ _____

FIGURE 3.1: Start-Up Costs Worksheet, continued

Office supplies $ _____

Renovations and improvements $ _____

Fixed tools and equipment $ _____

Portable tools and equipment $ _____

Other _____ $ _____

         Subtotal C $ _____

D. Transportation

Upfront cost to buy/lease transportation $ _____

Registration $ _____

Insurance $ _____

Special accessories $ _____

Other _____ $ _____

         Subtotal D $ _____

E. Web Site

Domain registration $ _____

Site development fees $ _____

Search engine and directory $ _____

Equipment $ _____

Software $ _____

Content and web tools $ _____

Hosting $ _____

Other _____ $ _____

         Subtotal E $ _____

F. Marketing

Research and planning costs $ _____

Signs $ _____

Brochures and fliers $ _____

Catalogs $ _____

FIGURE 3.1: Start-Up Costs Worksheet, continued

Initial advertising budget $ _____

Initial online promotion budget $ _____

Product samples $ _____

Other _____ $ _____

                              Subtotal F $ _____

G. Product Inventory (if applicable)

\# 1 _____ $ _____

\# 2 _____ $ _____

\# 3 _____ $ _____

\# 4 _____ $ _____

\# 5 _____ $ _____

                              Subtotal G $ _____

H. Adding Up the Costs

Business setup $ _____

Business identity $ _____

Office $ _____

Transportation $ _____

Web site $ _____

Marketing $ _____

Inventory $ _____

Total start-up costs $ _____

Working capital $ _____

Total investment needed $ _____

Building a Business Team

Building a business team is just as important as any other piece of the small business puzzle. Depending on the type of moneymaking enterprise you start and the products and services you sell, your business team might include family members, employees, and suppliers.

Family

Family members make up the first part of your business team, especially the ones who will also be working in the business with you. Even family members that do not work in the business will be affected by the business; it is inevitable. Consequently, you need to gain the support of the family for your venture, especially your parents.

Employees

Depending on the products or services you sell and your business goals, you may or may not need to hire employees. Employing people adds additional administrative and management work, but if your plans are to grow your business, at some point you will need to hire employees. The trick is to hire the right people. What are the characteristics of a good employee? Good employees are productive, project a professional image, are honest, loyal, confident, punctual, and can work with minimal supervision.

There are alternatives to employing people, such as hiring temporary workers to meet short-term labor requirements, which is a good choice. The cost is more expensive per hour on average than you would have to pay if you hired an employee, but when you factor in the time saved by not having to run help wanted ads, interview candidates, and check work references, the difference is negligible.

If you decide that hiring employees is the best option, you will have to comply with laws and regulations governing employment practices, including, but not limited to, labor laws, minimum wages, health and safety workplace issues, work hours, and workers' compensation insurance coverage. As an employer, you will need to obtain an Employer Identification Number (EIN), and you are also required to withhold and remit employee income tax and Social Security Insurance. Labor laws may be researched in the United States by contacting the Department of Labor, ☎ (877) 889-5627, ♂ www.dol.gov. In Canada, you can contact Human Resources Development Canada, ☎ (800) 567-6866, ♂ www.hrdc-drhc .gc.ca. To obtain an Employer Identification Number in the United States, visit your local Internal Revenue Service office or visit the IRS web site, ♂ www.irs.gov, to download the EIN form. In Canada, you can visit your local Canada Customs and Revenue Agency office or visit the CCRA web site, ✐ www.ccra-adrc.gc.ca, to download the EIN form.

Working with Suppliers

Suppliers are the other businesses that you purchase products and services from; they are also important members of your business team. Suppliers can play a major role in your ultimate success or failure. Consequently, these relationships need to be carefully developed and managed. Decisions to select and work with one supplier over another cannot be based solely on who offers the lowest price; you also have to factor many other influences, such as payment terms, warranties and guarantees, and reliability. Your supplier's promises to you are your promises to your customers. If your supplier lets you down, you in turn let your customers down.

When selecting suppliers find out what tools, equipment, or marketing materials they offer for free, or at greatly reduced costs to help their vendors. Many have programs in place in which they offer their trade accounts valuable equipment, marketing materials, and cooperative advertising opportunities that will help businesses to be more efficient, productive, and profitable. Items that you might be able to tap your suppliers for include ongoing specialized training, advertising specialties such as pens, product samples, contest prizes, signs, brochures and fliers, technical support, customer service support, computer hardware, software, and specialized tools and equipment. You never know unless you ask.

Developing a Business Image

You should plan to create a business image to help brand your business, products, and services, as well as to project a positive image, especially if you plan on growing your new business. Concentrate on three areas: logos and slogans, print identity, and uniforms.

Logos and Slogans

Attention-grabbing logos (like the Nike "swoosh" or MacIntosh computer's apple) and slogans (Nike's "Just Do It," for example) help build consumer awareness of your business, products, and services and project a positive business image. Business logos and promotional slogans play a major role in branding, which is a broad marketing term meaning getting people to instantly remember your product or service instead of the competitions'. This is especially true of logos because of their visual recognition qualities—consumers see instantly that it is a brand they know, like, and trust. To develop a slogan, simply think about the biggest benefit people receive from buying your products or services, and create a brief, yet powerful slogan around that benefit. Logos can be a little trickier to create unless you have design experience and a creative flair. But don't worry, if these are skills you lack, there are many logo design services such as The Logo Company, ♂ www.thelogocompany.com, and Logo Bee, ♂ www.logobee.com that can help you create a professional logo for your business, with prices for basic design services starting at less than $100.

Once you have decided on a logo design and a promotional slogan, you must consistently incorporate these into every area of your business, including stationery, signage, promotional materials, uniforms, and advertising. The more often consumers are exposed to your brand through the consistent use of logos and slogans, the more they will remember it, giving your business, products, and services brand recognition.

Print Identity Package

An identity package is comprised of the various print elements that you use daily in the course of operating your business—business cards, stationery, receipts, envelopes, estimate forms, presentation folders, marketing brochures, catalogs, fliers, and account statements. Key to a great print identity package is consistency. Develop a standard color scheme and font and combine these with your logo and slogan and use this all the time so that customers and prospects begin to visually link your business with your identity program. Always get three quotes for all of your printing needs, and do not necessarily buy based only on price. Instead, base your purchasing decision on quality, value, reputation, and turnaround time. In addition to your community printer, there are also many printers doing business online such as Print USA, ♂ www.printusa.com, which offers free quotes on a wide variety of products.

Uniforms

Top businesspeople have long understood the benefits associated with uniforms emblazoned with their business name and logo. These benefits include branding the business name, products, and services, as well as projecting a professional image. Uniforms also happen to be terrific advertising and promotional tools, especially T-shirts that only cost about $10 each and can be given to customers and through special promotions. In fact, great-looking uniforms do not have to be expensive; for as little as $20 each you can purchase smart casual golf shirts silk-screened or embroidered with your business name and logo. Hats start at $10 each, and jackets at about $50, all of which is money wisely spent to project a professional image and advertise your business.

Taking Your Moneymaking Venture Online

If you are excited about the idea of selling your products and services online, you should be. American consumers spent more than $95 billion on online purchases in 2003, and that number is expected to grow to $230 billion by 2008! Granted, products account for the larger portion of online sales, but many entrepreneurs also sell services online. There is a lot to know and learn about taking your business online and selling your products and services to e-consumers around the globe. Space restrictions do not allow for an in-depth explanation about everything you need to know about doing business online, but the following information covers the basics: building a web site, choosing a domain name, and search engine registration.

Building a Web Site

Your first decision will be to determine if you need a web site. Even if you are not planning to sell your products or services online, a web site can still be a very effective communication tool and be used for gathering information captured from visitors for research, planning, and marketing purposes. Ultimately, you will have to decide if the time and money spent to develop, maintain, and market a web site will be a wise investment and help you to meet your objectives. If you do decide to sell your products and services online, the advantages are apparent—the ability to sell 24 hours a day, communicate with prospects and customers quickly and cheaply, update your marketing message and special promotions almost instantly, and sell to consumers around the globe.

Once you have made the decision to build a web site, there are many subsequent decisions to be made: How much will it cost to create a web site? Who will build it? Who will maintain it? Who will host your site? What purchase payment options will you provide customers? And how will the site be promoted? The first option is to design, build, and maintain your own web site. There are numerous web site building programs available to enable novice Webmasters to build and maintain their own sites, but you will still need to be familiar with computers and the internet if you go this route. Hosting and maintenance costs will vary depending on the services you select—e-commerce shopping carts, payments systems, order tracking, content, web tools, and database storage options. Expect to pay a minimum of $20 per month for basic business web site hosting and about $250 per month for premium services.

The second option is to hire a professional to design and build your web site. Costs here have dramatically decreased in the past few years. In fact, for less than $500, you can have a complete, fully functional web site built with e-commerce, visitor interaction, and database marketing options. Click onto the Web Design Developers Association, ♂ www.wdda.org, to locate a web designer in your area, or consult your local Yellow Pages for web developers in your community.

Choosing a Domain Name

Selecting a domain name for your new web site or web business requires careful consideration because the domain name you select must be suited to the products and services you sell. This is often easier said than done. There are various domain extensions that can be used, such as .com, .biz, and .tv, or a country domain extension such as .ca in Canada and .us in the United States, but .com is still king in terms of online business and good dotcom designations are becoming increasingly difficult to acquire. The domain name you choose should be short, easy to remember, and easy to spell. Start the process of choosing a domain name right away, and register a few variations as soon as you have compiled a short list. Domain name registration fees vary depending on the designation and the registration service you choose, but expect to pay from a low of $10 per year for using a budget registrar, to as much as $75 per year with a full-service registration company. Most registrars also offer discounts if you register a name for a longer period—up to ten years. The majority of domain registration services also provide various additional internet and e-commerce services and packages, ranging from web site design to shopping carts, hosting and maintenance services, and web site promotional services. A few of the more popular domain name registration services include Domain Direct, ♂ www.domaindirect.com, Register, ♂ www.register.com, Go Daddy, ♂ www.godaddy.com, and Network Solutions, ♂ www.networksolutions.com.

Search Engine Registration

Because you don't know which search engine or directory people will use when looking for products and services online, you will need to register your web site and pages with numerous engines and directories to ensure maximum exposure. Registering with engines and directories can be very frustrating and time consuming because there are no standard guidelines, as most searches engines and directories have individual submission policies. There are search engine and directory submission services that will automatically submit or register your web site to all major search engines and directories, which is a wise choice for young entrepreneurs on a tight time schedule. Most of these services require that you only complete one relativity basic form, and they will do the rest. Some submission services are free, but the majority charge fees if you want quick listings, regular maintenance, and other premium listing services. These services offer small business owners with limited time to optimize their web sites for the best search ranks for a relatively small fee. The more popular submission services include Add Me, ♂ www.addme.com, Submit It, ♂ www.submit-it.com, and Submit Express, ♂ www.submitexpress.com. Google, ♂ www.google.com is the most widely known search engine, while Yahoo, ♂ www.yahoo.com is the most widely know search directory.

Pricing Products and Services

If your prices are too high, you will probably meet with resistance selling your products or services. If your prices are too low, you may also meet resistance selling your products and services because of perceived quality issues, or worse, lose money on each sale. Factors influencing pricing formulas include costs associated with the delivery of services, costs associated with the manufacturing of a product, or wholesale product costs, as well as fixed operating overheads, marketplace economic conditions, competition in the marketplace, consumer demand, seasonal pressures, political pressures, psychological factors, and how you want to position your products or services in the marketplace. As you can see, there are lots of factors that can affect the prices you charge for your goods and services.

A significant pricing concept to keep in mind when setting prices is that consumers see prices in very clearly defined terms: the price that you charge for your product or service versus how the product or service will fill their needs and provide value. When your pricing is correct, consumers don't think twice because they feel the price is fair in comparison to the value and benefits derived from the product or service. However, as soon as your price goes below or above the threshold of what consumers feel is in the fair range, you will meet resistance to the purchase. At this point, consumers must begin to justify why they will make the purchase, and you never want anyone to have to convince themselves to buy.

Competitive Pricing

A competitive pricing formula means that you find out how much competitors charge for their products and services, and charge more or less depending on how you want to position your business, products, and services in the marketplace. The downside to a competitive pricing formula is that it is not scientific. Your costs may be more or less than your competitor's costs, although chances are your costs will be less, and what may be a profitable price point for one business may not be for another charging the same price. You can find out how much your competition is charging by "mystery shopping" their businesses: becoming a customer, asking pricing questions, from advertisements and price lists, and from information posted on their web sites. If you use competitors' prices to determine your own prices, it is best to create unique competitive advantages to distinguish your products and services from theirs.

Cost Plus Pricing

The best way to determine the prices you will charge for your products or services is to use a cost-plus-pricing formula. To accomplish this you have to figure out your fixed operating costs, your variable costs associated with the delivery of services, the manufacturing of products, or the wholesale costs of products, and add a profit. The formula is:

$$\text{variable costs} + \text{fixed costs} + \text{profit} = \text{selling price.}$$

The first step is to determine how much money you need and want to earn per hour. The second step is to calculate your fixed costs, which are business expenses that do not fluctuate regardless of the amount of sales you make such as the telephone, rent, and insurance. The third step is to determine the costs incurred in making a product or buying products for resale and the costs associated with selling these products. The final step is to calculate and add a profit. Every business needs to generate a profit in order to stay in business and stay competitive in the marketplace. Most small business owners use a percentage to calculate a profit, such as total costs plus 20 percent.

Product Packaging, Delivery, and Inventory Management

Young people manufacturing or reselling products have to give thought to developing effective product packaging, product delivery options, and an inventory management system. Service providers are generally off the hook on the first two, but if you will also be installing products, you will need to create an inventory management system. All three are important issues and can negatively effective bottom line profits if they are not properly planned for, implemented, and managed.

Product Packaging

If you are going to manufacture a product or purchase products in bulk for resale, you will need to design and make product packaging, or have it professionally designed and made. You have to think of your product packaging as the silent salesperson. It doesn't talk, but it speaks volumes about your product, and more important, why people should buy it. Great packaging is like a great advertisement—it grabs attention, builds interest, creates desire, and motivates consumers to buy. Mediocre packaging can kill a great product, while incredible packaging can sell a mediocre product. What would you tell people face to face if you were trying to persuade them to buy your product? Your answer should be on your packaging.

If you intend to wholesale, consign, or sell your products through an online retailer or from a retail storefront, you will also need to obtain a Universal Product Code, widely known as a bar code, and have this printed on your packaging or accompanying price tag. Subdivisions Inc., ☎ (310) 927-1644, ♂ www.buyabar code.com sells and registers bar codes. At the time of this writing, each bar code costs $35, plus a one-time registration fee of $75.

Product Delivery

Product delivery issues must also be considered. There are numerous options available for how you get your products from point A to point B. You can deliver products, hire a delivery service, contract with a courier, uses airfreight services, or, if your products are small, rely on the postal system. Decisions are typically based on factors such as quantity, cost, schedule, and the type of product(s) being delivered. Regardless of the delivery method, costs vary depending on product weight, overall dimensions, schedule, geography, and insurable value.

You will also need to consider how you will pack items for transportation and the costs of packing and shipping materials such as boxes, wooden containers or pallets, bubble wrap, envelopes, tape, Styrofoam® pellets, and plastic bags. Most courier and freight companies sell packing and shipping materials, but shop around because in small quantities, these are very expensive. Office supply stores like Office Depot, ♂ www.officedepot.com, generally have lower costs on packing and shipping supplies; the lowest costs are found at packaging wholesalers.

Delivery costs and related supplies will have to be calculated and added to product pricing. All of the major courier and freight companies, such as Fed Ex, ♂ www.fedex.com, and UPS, ♂ www.ups.com, as well as the U.S. Postal Service, ♂ www.usps.com, and Canada Post, ♂ www.canadapost.ca, have software that automatically calculates shipping charges based on the information you enter. A few other benefits of this software are that it allows you to print customer labels, track packages, and automatically arrange for pickups and deliveries.

Inventory Management

You also have to give thought to how you will manage your inventory. This is not a big concern if you are manufacturing and selling products one at a time or in small quantities, or if you are buying individual products and selling these one at a time. Simply invest in a spiral notebook, create a few columns for product description and units, and you are pretty much set. Likewise, you can also create your own basic inventory management system using your computer and a spreadsheet program such as Excel.

However, if you are a mid- to large-volume product manufacturer or seller with numerous distribution channels, you will need a much more sophisticated inventory management system. Chances are you will need to invest in inventory management software with features such as customer database options, invoice creation, label making, inventory tracking, bar code scanning, tax codes, and automatic inventory reordering. Prices for inventory management software vary depending on features and peripherals, such as fixed and wireless scanners. You can search online business software directories like Soft Scout, ♂ www.soft scout.com, and The Software Network, ♂ www.thesoftwarenetwork.com, to find appropriate inventory management software.

Another aspect of inventory management is physical: You need a place to put your inventory, preferably a location that is easily accessed, dry, and secure, as well as apparatus such as shelving or bins to hold raw and finished products. If you do not have space at home, you will need to rent space, and security, cost, size, and proximity to your home will all need to be considered in terms of off-site storage. Public mini storage services are one of the best storage alternatives because you are not tied to long-term leases, and you don't have to worry about utilities and maintenance because that is included in the rent.

4

SALES, ADVERTISING, AND CUSTOMER SERVICE

This chapter is devoted sales, advertising, and how to provide great customer service. You will learn how to sell your products and services from home, a retail location, online, and at community events such as flea markets. If you manufacture or import products, you will also learn how to sell these wholesale and on consignment. Keep in mind that many of the sales and marketing ideas in this chapter are portable—most merchandising and selling techniques that work for homebased showrooms will also work at flea markets, for example.

Selling Basics

Sales success is a combination of education, practice, persistence, building on your strengths, and duplicating what gets the best results. So don't worry if selling is not your strongest skill; in time you will develop a technique that works for you. That said, preparation is the starting point for all selling. You have to know what you are selling inside out and upside down, and how customers benefit by purchasing and using your products or services. Product and service knowledge can be acquired through research, training, your suppliers, published information, and two of the most important methods: feedback from customers and hands-on experience. You must also know your target audience inside out and upside down; these are the people who need and want to buy the products and services you sell.

Being prepared also means you know your competition thoroughly—what people like and dislike about their products, services, prices, and warranties. You will also need to make sure that you have a toolbox packed with great sales tools. Think of your sales tools as the instruments you will use to grab peoples' attention, create buying desire, and most important, motivate them to take action and buy. Depending on the products and services you sell, sales tools can include promotional literature, product samples, attention-grabbing signage, customer testimonials, ironclad guarantees, or value-added promotions.

Selling Products and Services from Home

One of the advantages of selling products or services from home is it can be combined with many other sales methods—online sales, trade or consumer shows, or flea markets. Of course, selling from home will ultimately be determined by two issues: parental permission and the types of products or services you plan to sell. Not every home is suitable for product and service sales, and some communities do not allow or have restrictions in place for homebased businesses. Therefore, if you choose this route, a trip to the planning department's office at city hall will be required to find out the regulations in your area.

Homebased entrepreneurs have lots of options in terms of establishing an interior showroom to showcase and sell products such as fashion clothing and services such as web design. You can convert a garage, basement, den, or just about any room into a well-stocked showroom to peddle your products, or an office to meet with clients and discuss or provide services. Ideally the space you choose will have a separate entrance to provide privacy for family and customers alike. Also, even though this is your home, be sure to take advantage of proper display cases, racks, lighting, mirrors, and signage, and renovate and decorate the showroom or office to project the appropriate image for your business, products, and services.

Exterior display is also a good option for product sellers because of increased interest from passing motorists and pedestrians who will see your products as they pass by. Perfect products to display outdoors include lawn and garden products, vegetables, sporting goods, and craft items. Keep in mind that theft can become problematic when displaying products outdoors, so be sure to install motion lights, fencing, and gates as required. Like an interior showroom you also have to consider the image you want to project for your business; things such as peeling paint, overgrown gardens, and broken windows will all have a negative impact on business. Before displaying products for sale, make sure to spruce up the exterior and make repairs as necessary, and keep on top of maintenance.

There is a lot to know about operating a business from home so you might want to get a copy of *Entrepreneur Magazine's Ultimate Homebased Business Handbook* (Entrepreneur Press, 2004) from the library or bookstore. The book is an *A to Z* explanation about everything you need to know about starting and operating a homebased business. Likewise, Small Office Home Office (SOHO) is an organization comprised of small business owners that mainly operate their businesses from homebased locations. In the United States click on www.soho.org for more information, and in Canada click on www.soho.ca.

Vending Kiosks and Carts

If selling products from home is not an option, perhaps you will need to rent retail space. This doesn't have to be a whole storefront, other options such as a mall kiosk or vending cart represent great selling opportunities for young entrepreneurs with the right products. A few of the best products to sell from vending carts and kiosks include sunglasses, jewelry, watches, clothing, craft items, gift baskets, toys, candles, cosmetics, soaps, and specialty foods.

Kiosks and pushcarts are available in both interior and exterior styles, though the focus here is on interior kiosks and pushcarts that you would find in malls, office buildings, government buildings, airports, and train stations. Many of these carts and kiosks are available to rent on a short- or long-term basis, from one day, to an entire year. Generally speaking, it is the building or property management company that rents vending space. In addition to a vendor's permit, most locations also require you to have liability insurance. Locations such as the ones mentioned above can be lucrative in terms of revenues, but vendors who specialize in selling from mall kiosks tend to fare the best and produce the highest sales, especially during the Christmas shopping season. Carriage Works manufactures custom kiosks and pushcarts; they can be contacted at ☎ (541) 882-9661, or online at ♂ www.carriageworks.com. The Cart Owners Association of America is a good source of pushcart vending information. The association can be contacted at ☎ (559) 332-2229, or online at ♂ www.cartowners.org.

Selling Products Wholesale

Young entrepreneurs that manufacture products can sell their goods directly to consumers, or you can go after the big market opportunities and wholesale your products in mass quantities to independent retailers and chain retailers, or to middlemen, such as wholesalers and distributors. If you choose this route, there are basically three avenues available—grassroots wholesaling, established wholesalers, and the business-to-business trade shows. All three have advantages and disadvantages, and are discussed in greater detail below. Depending on your products, price points, and business and sales objectives, you may elect to combine one or more of these approaches to wholesale the products you make.

Grassroots Wholesaling

Grassroots wholesaling means setting appointments with independent and chain retailers, and armed with product samples and promotional literature, you present and pitch your products with the goal of the retailer purchasing and stocking your products in their store(s). Securing appointments with independent retailers is not difficult, and generally only requires a telephone call or introduction letter to get the ball rolling.

Chain retailers, however, are an entirely different ball game because all buying decisions are made at the head office level, regardless if the retailer is a franchise operation or not. It can be very difficult to get past the gatekeepers and to the people that make buying decisions; if you do get five minutes of their time, you better have something very impressive to pitch! Chain retailers want to know why they should buy your products, what the competitive advantages and special features are, and how their customers benefit by purchasing them. They also want to know how you are going to promote the product to motivate consumers to go to the retailers' stores and buy. It is possible to land vendor accounts with major chain retailers, but be prepared to work hard and smart to accomplish this goal.

Established Wholesalers

This is much like the grassroots approach, but instead of setting appointments with retailers, you set appointments with businesses that already have established channels of distribution in place, namely wholesalers and distributors. In a nut-shell, you sell your product to the wholesaler, who in turns sells it to the retailer, who in turn sells it to the consumer. The major downside with this sales option is price point. You have to have the ability to sell your product for drastically less than retail, often by as much as 60 percent off retail, in order for the wholesaler to be able to sell to retailers at a profitable price point. But with that said, you can make up lower profits per unit by selling in larger quantities. A good starting point is to contact the National Association of Wholesale-Distributors, ☎ (202) 872-0885 ♪ www.naw.org, to find wholesalers selling the types of products you make to retailers.

Business-to-Business Trade Shows

To land retailer accounts for the products you make, the best approach is to exhibit at business-to-business trade shows, which means that businesses display and sell their products and services to other businesses and not to the general public. Business-to-business trade shows are basically the same as consumer trade shows (which are businesses selling to the general public) with one big exception; wholesale buyers representing national and international retailers of all sizes attend, and they are there to find new products to buy in quantity. There are industry trade shows for just about every type of product imaginable—craft products, fashions and accessories, furniture, garden products, food products, recreational products, and more. Best of all, unlike consumer shows, trade show buyers do not want to purchase products and take immediate delivery; they are there to scout products, negotiate prices, and place orders for future delivery. Therefore, all you have to bring are product samples and a catalog listing your products, accompanied by order forms indicating unit pricing, bulk pricing, payment terms and methods, delivery schedules, minimum order amounts, warranty information, and return policy.

The National Mail Order Association, ☎ (612) 788-4197 ♪ www.nmoa.org, publishes an annual Industry Trade Show, Importer, and Wholesale Marketplace Directory, which includes listing information on more than 150 product trade shows, as well as wholesale publications, trade magazines, and manufacturer directories.

Selling Products on Consignment

Consignment means that you place the products you make into retail stores and get paid only if the product(s) are sold. Consigning the products that you make with retailers can be a viable way to get your products into stores and ultimately purchased by consumers. However, consignment is not suited to all products, and there are additional drawbacks such as high sales commission fees, loss of control over merchandising, and having to sometimes wait long periods of time to be paid on sales.

Some of the products for consignment include items such as craft products, art, gift products, woodcrafts, designer fashions, and other handcrafted products. If you decide to go the consignment route, there are four points to consider: the types of retailers and location, the consignment agreement, merchandising and pricing, and inventory management and product delivery.

Selecting Retailers

Not all retailers will agree to sell your products on consignment, but many will, especially those selling gift and craft products. Select wisely and make sure your products are compatible with the types of products the retailer sells. Likewise, you also have to decide if you will consign with local retailers as well as out-of-town retailers. Consigning locally is very convenient, easy to ship and monitor inventory, while out-of-town consignments add travel time and/or shipping costs. That said, consigning out of your local area opens the possibility of selling more products to a broader audience of consumers. Overall, when selecting retailers to consign with, consider the types of products they sell, their current sales, their reputation, and if they have an established consignment program in place.

Consignment Agreement

The devil is always in the details, so you must always scrutinize all consignment agreements before signing and stocking products. How much is the retailer's sales commission? Depending on the value of the product, expect the retailer to retain a commission in the range of 25 to 50 percent. Does the retailer generate a consignment sales report? How often do you get paid? How is the payment made—check, direct deposit, or cash? Ideally, you want a formal sales report, and to be paid by check every 30 days for the previous month's sales. What are the retailer's policies in terms of consignment product returns, refunds, and theft? Does the retailer's insurance cover your products in the event of fire, flood, or other causes of damage? Returns and refunds are inevitable. You will need to come to a mutually agreeable policy. In terms of theft or damage to stock while in the retailer's possession, it is their liability, not yours. Make sure that this is included in the consignment agreement.

Merchandising and Pricing

Merchandising refers to how you display your products and attract the attention of customers. In a perfect consignment situation, you want the ability to merchandise and price your products in each location. Unfortunately this is not always possible. Many retailers reserve the right to decide how consigned products will be merchandised inside the store, as well as the retail selling price. I believe the right to merchandise and price your products is the key to successful and profitable consigning. Fight for this right, but at the same time go armed with the tools needed to persuade retailers to your way of thinking. These tools include a high-quality in-demand product, competitive pricing, and attention grabbing packaging and merchandise displays. You also want to fight for the best real estate inside the store—close to the cash checkout, at the entrance, and/or good window visibility are the best locations inside most retail stores. Retailers are in the business of selling not simply displaying products. You have to develop products and merchandising strategies that will motivate consumers to buy.

Inventory Management and Product Delivery

You also need to develop a standardized inventory management system, especially if you consign products with more than one retailer. The simplest way is to create a consignment form listing initial inventory stocked in each location, and removing items as they are sold or removed from the store, as well as listing new products each time they are stocked. It is crucial to keep an accurate record of all inventory, as well as obtain signatures from retailers every time products are restocked or removed from the store. Not only will this protect against inventory "shrinkage," but also over time you will be able to determine what products sell best at each of the retailers, and at what times of year, enabling you to develop marketing strategies to maximize sales at each location. You will also have to think about product delivery. Will you hand deliver to all consignment accounts or have products shipped? If your accounts are close and you have access to transportation, you can deliver: if not, it will probably be cheaper to have products shipped, in which case you have to find out how much this will add to the unit cost of each product and either price accordingly or decide if you are going to charge shipping (probably not much of an option with consignment).

Selling Products and Services Online

Even though determined young entrepreneurs have many options for promoting and selling products and services online, the following information focuses only on eBay and internet malls. The advantages of selling online are obvious—open 24-hours a day, trade information with customers in minutes, you can update your marketing message and strategy quickly, conveniently, and very inexpensively, and the rent is cheap.

eBay

Online auction and retail marketplace giant eBay, ♂ www.ebay.com, has more than 100 million registered users around the globe, has set up camp in more than 20 countries worldwide, and even more amazing, 450,000 of eBay's registered users claim selling products through eBay is their sole source of income! Volumes can, have, and will continue to be written on the subject of profiting from doing business on eBay, but space here does not permit a detailed explanation about how it all works. So I strongly suggest that you spend lots of time on eBay, take advantage of eBay-sponsored workshops, and read books about eBay selling to further your knowledge before you get started.

The most popular and common type of eBay auction is the traditional or classic auction. In this type of auction there is no reserve (lowest) price set, and at the end of the 1-, 3-, 5-, 7-, or 10-day auction, the highest bid wins. The theory of a short auction is it enables you to generate more heat and bidding excitement. A longer auction might eventually lead to diminished interest as time passes, although, a longer auction also means your product(s) will be exposed to more potential buyers and might fetch a higher price. Ultimately, you will have to play around with auction lengths a bit to find what works best for what you sell. eBay also offers a *Buy it Now* option, which means you can set a price for your product, and a buyer can purchase it for the set price without having to wait for the auction to end. But, once you receive a bid, the *Buy It Now* icon disappears and the sale reverts back to a traditional auction.

Sellers also have the option to set a reserve price for the item for sale. A reserve price is the lowest possible price a seller is prepared to take for the item; buyers do not know how much the reserve price is, only that there is a reserve. Once a bid exceed the reserve price, the item sells to the highest bidder. If the reserve price is not met before the auction expires, the item does not sell and the seller can choose whether to relist the product. Many sellers like to set a reserve price matching their product cost as a way to protect against selling for less than cost.

Some useful eBay information sites are:

- eBay Learning Center, ♂ http://pages.ebay.com/education/index.html
- eBay Promotional Tools, ♂ http://pages.ebay.com/sellercentral/tools.html
- eBay Seller's Guide, ♂ http://pages.ebay.com/help/sell/index.html
- eBay Selling Internationally, ♂ http://pages.ebay.com/help/sell/ia/selling_internationally.html
- eBay Shipping Center, ♂ http://pages.ebay.com/services/buyandsell/shipping.html

- eBay Stores, ♂ http://pages.ebay.com/storefronts/start.html

Internet Malls

Just like bricks-and-mortar shopping malls, internet malls offer consumers a one-stop shopping opportunity for a wide range of products and services. There are a number of companies and services offering internet mall and e-storefront programs. The big players in are eBay, ♂ www.ebay.com, Amazon, ♂ www.amazon .com, and the Internet Mall, ♂ www.internetmall.com. There are also hundreds of smaller outfits offering numerous online selling opportunities for the small e-tailer, such as American Internet Mall, ♂ www.aimone.com, Canadian Internet Mall, ♂ www.cdn-mall.com, and Mall Park, ♂ www.mallpark.com.

Most internet malls or e-storefront programs offer two basic types of services. One, they operate as a directory service listing product and/or service categories; for a fee your business can be listed under one or more appropriate categories. Taking advantage of this option means you need a web site so you can link to the mall's directory. Two, some internet malls and e-storefront services offer a more complete package, which can include one or more of the following: domain name registration, web site building, hosting, e-commerce tools, back-end administration tools (web stats and database management, for instance), and promotion. There are also programs that blend the two types according to your needs and budget. Fees vary widely depending on your level of participation and the services you need, but generally start at a few hundred dollars in development fees along with ongoing monthly fees ranging from $20 to $500. But before signing on the dotted line, do your homework to ensure the mall has a good reputation with vendors and shoppers, offers the services you need, attracts your target audience, and has a strong marketing campaign in place to promote the mall and participating vendors.

Selling Products and Services at Events

In addition to selling products and services from home, retail locations, and online, there are also many special events that provide fantastic selling opportunities, including consumer shows, arts and crafts shows, flea markets, and community events.

Consumer Shows

The difference between trade and consumer shows is that trade shows are businesses exhibiting for and selling to other businesses, while consumer shows are for the general public to attend, browse, gain information, and shop. Consumer shows are a great way to showcase and sell your products or services to a large audience at one time, in one place, and in a very cost-effective manner. Depending on the show and duration, you have the potential to come in contact with hundreds, if not thousands, of people that are ready to buy. There are consumer shows for every imaginable type of product or service—home and garden shows, food shows, sports and recreation shows, gift shows, photography shows, baby shows, and on and on.

The consumer show pace can be fast and furious, and time is a commodity that is always in short supply. So it is important to have a well-rehearsed sales plan ready to put into action. When designing your booth and displays, keep in mind that booths alive with exciting product and service demonstrations draw considerably more interest and larger crowds then static booths, which generally equals more sales or more sales leads.

Arts and Craft Shows

Arts and crafts shows are an excellent forum for selling high-quality handmade products such as folk art, fine art, woodturnings, sewing and needlecraft specialties, soaps, candles, stained glass items, handmade toys, pottery, and jewelry. Shows range in size from small church-organized shows with a handful of vendors to international fine arts and crafts shows lasting for a week and drawing hundreds of vendors and thousands of consumers from around the globe. Although most are small events over a weekend and take place in community centers, exhibition buildings, hotels, convention centers, and school gymnasiums. Booth rents vary widely from $5 to $500 per day, depending on the size of the show and expected audience. It is always a good idea to visit larger and more expensive shows before signing on to vend to make sure the show and audience meet your exhibiting criteria, check out the competition, and talk to other vendors to get firsthand feedback about the show. Additional points to consider include admission fees, parking, competition, rent, operating history, and attendance statistics. Crafts Shows USA, ♂ www.craftshowsusa.com, provides a free online directory service listing information on hundreds of craft shows.

Once you have decide on a show, be sure to create a checklist to prepare for the event, and check off each item or task as completed so you are 100 percent ready to sell come show time.

Keep your booth, displays, and products, clean, organized, and use mirrors and lighting to brighten your sales space. Because shows can be very busy, price all items to save time repeating prices to everyone who asks. Also, create a couple of worthwhile *show specials*, such as "buy one, get one at half price," "free shipping on orders of $100 or more," or "free gift wrapping," to pull shoppers into your booth.

You will also need a receipt book, credit card slips (if applicable), calculator, pens, price gun or blank price tags, and a cash lockbox. Also bring along a basic toolbox stocked with a hammer, screwdrivers, flashlight, wrench, extra light bulbs, cleaner, rags, stapler, and garbage bags. And bring lots of packing materials including newspaper, plastic bags, boxes, tape, string, and scissors. Associations such as the Arts and Crafts Association of America, ☎ (616) 874-1721 ♂ www.artsandcraftsassoc.com, and the Canadian Crafts and Hobby Association, ☎ (403) 291-0559 ♂ www.cdncraft.org, also provide lots of information about selling products at arts and crafts shows.

Flea Markets

Did you know that many flea market vendors are earning as much as $50,000 a year working only a two days a week? Did you also know that there are an estimated 750,000 flea market vendors peddling products in the United States and Canada at more than 10,000 flea markets, bazaars, and swap meets, and some draw crowds in excess of 25,000 people a day? Needless to say, if you choose to sell new or used products at flea markets you'll be in good company and have the potential to earn excellent profits.

Flea markets are everywhere, but before selecting one, visit a few first to get a feel for the venue, vendors, and visitors. Check out the venue—do they charge admission, is there adequate parking, and do they heavily promote the event? Check out the vendors—what do they sell, how much are they charging, how much are they selling, and how many are selling the same things as you? Check out the visitors—are they buying or browsing, how many are there, and do they meet your target customer profile?

There are also many types of flea markets—weekends only, every day, summer only, outside under tent, open air, and inside events, and all have advantages and disadvantages. Booth rents also vary widely from a low of $5 per day to as much as $100 for single-day events. When selecting a flea market, also look for adequate customer and vendor parking, electricity, phone lines for credit card and debit card terminals, on-site ATM machine, washrooms, food services, and excellent overall organization. You will also need to supply your own transportation and equipment such as dollies to load and unload merchandise and displays. Some flea markets provide merchandising tables, canopies, and displays, while others rent these items separately, and still others do not supply anything except for the booth, so be sure to find out up front.

Always remember that everyone shopping at flea markets expects to bargain and wants to flex her negotiation muscle, so be ready to haggle. Price items 10 to 20 percent higher so you have room to negotiate, yet still get your price. To find flea markets, use online directories like Flea USA, ♂ www.flea markets.com, Flea Market Guide, ♂ www.fleamarketguide.com, and Keys Flea Market, ♂ www.keysfleamarket.com. All list hundreds of flea markets index geographically.

Community Events

Every community throughout North America has numerous events and celebrations each year, such as parades, fairs, holiday celebrations, farmers' markets, public markets, rodeos, music festivals, and swap meets. Many of these events provide excellent opportunities to sell all sorts of products—art, jewelry, sunglasses, watches, pottery, clothing, candles, soaps, silk-screened T-shirts, handbags, toys, tools, craft items, and specialty foods, just to mention a few. Booth fees and permit costs vary depending on the type of event, anticipated crowd, and duration of the event. Some are free, but most charge. The most expensive are usually fairs and exhibitions, which can cost as much as $500 a day, but most events charge less than $50 for vending space.

Selling at community events is like any other retailing opportunity—think booth location within the event, signage, professional displays, quality merchandise, fair pricing, quick service, and a smile. Also, be sure to print fliers describing your products and how people can contact you after the event, including web address, e-mail, and telephone number. The fliers should be given to people who purchase products, and to people just looking, because there is the potential they will become customers at a later date.

Advertising Basics

Advertising is a tool that can drive consumers in mass numbers to your business to buy products and services. Adversely, advertising can be a complete waste of time and money. Young entrepreneurs with limited advertising budgets have to make researched and informed decisions when it comes to allocating precious money to advertising activities. Creating great advertising is comprised of many elements—attention-grabbing headlines, powerful images, incredible offers, and a call to action. This is referred to as the AIDA advertising formula—attention, interest, desire, and action. Even if you plan on doing little in the way of traditional advertising in newspapers for instance, you still need the ability to create convincing advertising and sales copy for use in packaging, sales letters, catalogs, fliers, newsletters, signage, or web site content.

Newspaper Advertising

There are basically two types of newspaper advertising options—display advertising and classified advertising. For the majority of small businesses, classified advertising offers much greater value than display advertising for a few reasons. First, display advertising is very expensive, and placing only the occasional ad because of a limited budget does not work (special sales or promotional events excluded). You need repetition in order to build long-term beneficial awareness of your business, products, and services. Further, most newspapers are jammed cover-to-cover with display advertisements leaving your ad fighting with hundreds of other ads to capture the readers' attention. If you opt to buy display advertising space in newspapers, first ask for the media kit or card, which tells you about the newspaper' readers—who they are, where they come from, what they do for a living, their level of education, and how much money they make. This information will enable you to determine if the newspaper's target audience is your target audience.

Classified advertising, on the other hand, is unquestionably one of the best advertising options for young entrepreneurs. Not only are classified ads easy to create and cheap to run, but they almost always have a higher response rate than display advertisements because people generally read the classifieds looking for a specific product or service, not for entertainment. Because classified advertisements are cheap to run and quick to post, continually look for ways to improve your results by testing new ads in various publications. Test your headline, your main sales message, and your special offers on a regular basis. Classified advertising rates vary by publication, number of words, number of insertions, and other factors such as the use of icons, borders, and photographs—which, by the way, almost always increase response rates, making the extra cost a very wise expenditure.

Online Advertising

There are a number of ways to advertise products and services online. In fact, there are so many online promotional methods that many books have been written solely on the topic, but space here limits us to discussing the basics, which are banner advertising, e-publications, and pay-per-click programs.

Advertising banners are a very popular way to promote products and services and drive traffic to your web site or online location where your products or services can be purchased. Depending on the target audience you want to reach, banner advertising costs range from a few dollars per thousand "impressions" to a few hundred dollars per thousand impressions. The lure of low cost banner advertising might be tempting, but results can suffer dramatically by not presenting your advertising message to your primary target audience. Bigger is not always better. Mega web sites may attract thousands, if not, millions of visitors, but that does not necessarily mean they are comprised of your target audience.

Advertising in electronic publications (ezines) can also be a highly effective way to reach your target audience at a very modest cost. Before committing to advertising, find out audience size, demographics, and advertising costs. Again, bigger is not necessarily better, because these publications often contain more advertisements. Your main consideration should always be based on reaching your target audience. Ezine Listings, ♂ www.ezinelistings.com, which list electronic publications indexed by subject, and Ezine Directory, ♂ www.news letter-directory.com, list thousands of electronic publications indexed by subject.

Pay-per-click programs are another highly effective form of online advertising, which involves bidding on priority keywords you believe your target audience uses to search for the products or services you sell. Google's AdWords, ♂ www .adwords.google.com, and Overture's Pay-For-Performance, ♂ www.over ture.com, are the big players in pay-per-click advertising. Each has different requirements and rules for keyword selection, but both are similar in the way you bid for keywords. For instance, you can bid one dollar for a specific keyword and if you are the highest bid, you win and get top search results rankings. On the other hand, if you bid 20 cents and someone else bids more for the same keywords, your ranking will be greatly reduced. You are charged this fee anytime someone clicks on your ad and is relocated to your web site or e-storefront.

Promotional Fliers

Promotional fliers represent one of the best and most cost effective methods of advertising available to young business owners. You should take the time needed to learn basic desktop publishing skills and purchase computer hardware and desktop publishing software programs such as those offered by Adobe, ♂ www.adobe.com, and Corel, ♂ www.corel.com, so you have the ability to design and produce your fliers in house. In addition to saving money, having the ability to create your own fliers also saves time because you can create promotional materials and be ready to use them on the same day, instead of waiting days or weeks working around a print shop's schedule. Once your fliers have been created, they can be copied in bulk for as little as two cents each at your local copy center, or you can invest in a high-speed laser printer and print them yourself.

The great benefit of printed promotional fliers is that they can be used everywhere and for everything, even as a replacement in most cases for a business card. Hand them out at flea markets, trade shows, and networking meetings.Hire your friends to canvas busy parking lots tucking fliers underneath windshield wipers and leave them in public spaces and on transit for riders to read and take home. First check rules in your area. Some municipalities require you to purchase a permit to hand out fliers in transit stations and other public places.

Signs

Signs are another low-cost, high-impact form of advertising because they work to promote your products and services 24 hours a day, 365 days a year, for free, making them an important investment for all businesses. Signs should be professionally designed and constructed because you always want to make a positive first impression and project an appropriate image. Faded signs, peeling paint, torn banners, or signs that require any sort of maintenance or look homemade in general send out negative messages about your business and the products or services you sell.

Chances are you also need to buy various types of signs for numerous uses, such as event signage and banners to use at flea markets, consumer shows, and community events. Portable promotional signage should also be professionally designed and include attention-grabbing design elements such as vivid colors and images of the products you sell to lend visual description to perfectly describe your products and services at a glance. If you are going to use your vehicle for business, my advice is to sign it using magnetic or stick-on vinyl signs. I would not only sign the vehicle, I would also park in high-traffic locations when the car is not in use, even if this means feeding parking meters. Always think about maximizing the marketing value of these rolling billboards.

Customer Service Basics

When you stop to consider that it costs ten times as much to find a new customer as it does to keep a customer you already have, it makes perfect sense to keep all of your customers happy and buying. How do you keep your customers happy? By providing a quality product, service with a smile, appreciating your customers, and by standing behind your work.

One of the easiest customer service concepts to grasp is the simple fact that people like to do business with people they like. So it stands to reason that you should go out of your way to be likeable—smile, take an interest in your customers, treat them fairly, and thank them for their business. That's about all it takes to provide great customer service. Another easy customer service concept to master is to always fix the customer first instead of focusing on why a product doesn't work. Once you've fixed your customer, turn your attention to the source of the problem or complaint. Also keep in mind the vast majority of customer service complaints arise from mismatched expectations. It makes sense to reduce the potential for mismatched expectations between you and customers by reviewing all details of the sale prior to product or service delivery, and by asking customers their expectations. You need to know that your customers' expectations for the product or service are the same as yours.

Product and Service Warranties

Another important element of providing great customer service is to put your money where your mouth is and back up your claims of a high quality product or service by providing an ironclad warranty. Not only can an ironclad warranty be used to support your marketing claims, but you can also use your warranty to separate your products or services from competing products and services in the marketplace. For instance, if a competing product is warranted for one year, make yours two. Or, if competitors guarantee workmanship for 30 days, guarantee your workmanship for 60 days. Consumers have become very savvy and want to know that if the product malfunctions or breaks down for any reason, they have recourse to get the problem fixed. Yes, depending on the products you make or sell, or the services you provide there must be warranty terms and conditions to protect your business. But at the same time, every business making and selling products or providing services should strive to develop the strongest warranty possible.

Returns and Refunds

At some point you will have customers who want to return products, request a refund, or want to cancel a product or service order. All businesses, regardless of size, face returns, refunds, and canceled orders. Consequently, it is best to establish return, refund, and order cancellation policies before opening for business. The following are a few points you will need to consider:

- Will you allow customers to return products they have purchased from your business, or will all sales be final?
- In what condition will you allow products to be returned? Unused? Unwrapped?
- How long will your product return or refund policy be—7, 14, 30 days, or longer?

- Will you offer customers the option of exchanging products for similar products, a credit against future purchases, or an outright cash refund?

If you are going to provide refunds, make sure your policy corresponds with the payment method. If the customer paid in cash, offer a cash refund. If the customer paid with a credit card, you will need to credit his charge account. And, if a customer paid by check, make sure the check has cleared your bank before refunding any money.

The final consideration is product order cancellations. Most U.S. states and Canadian provinces have consumer protection mechanisms in place that enable consumers to cancel orders within a prescribed timeframe, which is generally referred to as a *cooling off period*. However, there is not a single standard time limit to this law. You will need to contact the SBA or your lawyer to inquire about your specific area and how the law is applied.

CHAPTER

5

MAKING AND SELLING SIMPLE PRODUCTS

Making and selling products truly knows no boundaries—any young person with a desire to earn extra money can make and sell a product, regardless of age, special skills, and business experience. We all know how to make something, or with basic training can quickly learn how to make a product(s) that can be sold for a profit. That is entirely the purpose of this chapter—to help you identify the best product(s) to make and sell for big profits.

There are also a number of beneficial advantages associated with making and selling products. A few of these include excellent part-time profit potential, small start-up investment, limited financial risk because the majority of funding will be used to secure raw materials, and the flexibility to work part time, seasonally, or just occasionally.

Seashell Crafts

Cashing in on the demand for seashell products such as shell wind chimes, shell-covered jewelry boxes, shell costume jewelry, and shell lamps is simple because shell craft products are easy to make, and even easier to sell. Why are seashell craft products easy to sell? Simply because few people can resist the call of the ocean, the lure of the beach, and the cry of the gull, all enjoyable images connected with seashell craft products. In addition to thinking about the type(s) of seashell products you are going to make and sell, you will also need a good supply of seashells, a glue gun, basic hand tools, and appropriate fasteners determined by the products you make. Combine these things with a bit of ingenious marketing savvy and you're in the seashell crafts manufacturing and sales business. There are many seashell wholesalers such as Sanibel Seashell ♂ www.seashells.com, Shell Horizons ♂ www.shellhorizons.com, and The Shell Store ♂ www.theshell store.com. All offer a wide variety of native shells and exotic seashells from around the world. Sell your beautiful seashell crafts creations online using eBay, internet malls, and craft malls, as well as offline on weekends and during holidays by renting space at flea markets, arts and crafts shows, church bazaars, and at community events like fairs and parades.

Basket Weaving

Making and selling baskets is the perfect part-time moneymaking opportunity for young entrepreneurs with a creative flair. Although basket making and weaving is a centuries-old craft, little has changed in the way handmade baskets are made, as they are still handwoven by the craftsperson. At one time baskets were used every day to carry goods and often as a system for measuring quantities of goods such as eggs, meat, vegetables, and bread. Baskets today are more artistic than utilitarian, which is reflected in the prices. It is not uncommon for highly artistic handcrafted baskets to fetch as much as $500. Learning to make baskets can be accomplished by teaching yourself the craft through trial and error and with the aid of instructional books and videos. Or you can enroll in basket-making classes, which are offered in just about every community through colleges, clubs, and private instruction. You will need to invest in basic tools such as a measuring tape, scissors, water bucket, awl, knife, and clamps, as well as basket-making materials.

Lots of information about basket making, supplies, and resources can be found online. A few of the better online sources include Basket Makers ☞ www.basket makers.org, Basket Makers Catalog, ☞ www.basketmakerscatalog.com, Basket Patterns, ☞ www.basketpatterns.com, and the Handweavers Guild of America ☞ www.weavespindye.org. Handcrafted baskets can be sold directly to consumers using online marketplaces such as eBay and internet craft and gift malls, or you can sell to consumers in the bricks and mortar world by renting booth space on weekend at flea markets, craft fairs, and gift shows.

Candle Making

Aromatherapy candles, scented jar candles, floating candles, wedding candles, novelty candles, 100 percent beeswax candles, citronella candles, and decorative bowl and crock candles are just a few of the different kinds of candles that you can easily make at home part-time and sell for big profits. The candle making learning curve is short, which makes this an excellent moneymaking opportunity for kids, teens, and young adults. The best way to start is to educate yourself about candles—how they are made, what the various uses are, and where you can buy the basic materials needed to start. Purchase candle-making books and videos, attend local candle-making classes offered by community centers, craft groups, continuing education programs, and candle-making studios, and partner with other hobby candle makers to learn the secrets of the craft. Sell your candle creations online utilizing eBay and internet malls. You can sell directly to friends, family members, and people in the neighborhood, as well as at flea markets and from vending carts at farmers' and public markets on weekends and holidays. Also, if you are really ambitious and want a shot at earning big bucks don't overlook the possibility of mass-producing candles so that you can establish wholesale accounts with gift and home décor retailers right across the county. Of course, keep safety in mind when making any product. Visit the National Candle Association online at ☞ www.candles.org, for additional information about making and selling candles.

Cactus Arrangements

For creative young entrepreneurs, making and selling unique cactus arrangements offers an excellent opportunity to earn a few extra dollars every week. Cactus arrangements make great gifts for home and office décor, and making them is easy. Collect things such as small rocks, gravel, pinecones, and small pieces of driftwood or bark, most of which can be obtained in small quantities for free if you are prepared to go for a hike in the woods or on the beach. Arrange these items with planted dwarf cactuses in terracotta or similar pots. That is about all that is required to make cactus arrangements. Sell the cactus arrangements online via specialty gift and gardening sites. You can also sell the cactus arrangements at craft, gift, Christmas, and gardening shows. If you get very creative and create unique arrangements, you can try to target potential volume buyers like corporations, small business owners, professionals, and salespeople who routinely send clients unique appreciation gifts. Books such as 📖 *The Complete Book of Cacti and Succulents*, Terry Hewit (DK Publishing, 1997), will teach you everything you need to know about cactus species. And, you can purchase cactus plants at wholesale prices from suppliers such as The Cactus Ranch ☎ (903) 567-5042, and Kactus Korral ☎ (830) 540-4521, ♂ www.kactus.com.

Soapy Profits

Making and selling specialty soaps is an easy and fun business for kids, teens, and young adults of all ages to start. You need to invest only a few dollars into basic soap making materials to get rolling. There are numerous types of specialty soaps that you can make and sell, like aromatherapy soaps, hypoallergenic soaps, dermatological soaps, novelty soaps, herbal soaps, and soap gift baskets sets. And, there are just as many ways to sell handmade specialty soaps. For instance, you can sell to friends, family, and neighbors, as well as organizing and hosting in-home soap sales parties. You can also sell your homemade soaps on online using eBay and internet malls, and offline by renting booth space at craft fairs, flea markets, and health and beauty shows, or by renting kiosk space in malls on weekends leading up to Christmas. And if you are really ambitious, you can also sell to retailers such as gift shops, bed and bath retailers, and natural health products retailers on a wholesale or consignment basis. There are lots of options. A good source of information about soap making can be found online at The Handcrafted Soap Makers Guild ♂ www.soapguild.org. There you will find helpful soap making and marketing information and resources.

Garden Stepping Stones

Making and selling garden stepping stones is simple, fun, suitable for all ages, and you can earn lots of extra money. The main supplies you need are molds, cement, reinforcement mesh, and items to decorate the surface such as tiles, glass, color stones, or embossed designs. All of the supplies needed are widely available, including through many online sources, such as Garden Molds and Supplies, *d* www.gardenmolds.com, and LaBrake's Garden Path *d* www.garden ponds.com/molds.htm. You can also make your own molds out of wood, plastic, or metal. There is not much involved in making stepping stones—fill the mold half full with concrete, lay in the reinforcing mesh, pour in the balance of the concrete, wait about 30 minutes to add decorations on top, and let dry for a couple days. Presto, a completed stepping stone ready to sell. In total, each costs approximately $2 to $3 to make, but sell in the range of $15 to $25 each, depending on size and complexity of design. Expect to sell wholesale to garden centers for about half of the retail sale price. In addition to wholesale sales, stepping stones can also be sold directly to consumers at gift shows, home and garden shows, craft fairs, online via internet malls and eBay, and at flea markets. Likewise, selling from home supported by signage and local advertising is a good idea because you can create elaborate stepping stone walkways to show customers and showcase the beauty and functionality of the product (providing your parents don't mind).

Birdhouses

Birdhouses are very easy to build, even for kids and young adults with limited, if any, carpentry skills. To get started building birdhouses you need design plans, a small workshop, and an assortment of basic power and hand tools (if you are a young teen, you will need to do the wood cutting part with an adult). There are even birdhouse kits available through most building centers that are precut and ready to assemble and paint. Because there are numerous types of birdhouses for various bird species, you will need to do a bit of research to pinpoint the types of birdhouses you will build. Also, consider using only recycled materials in the construction of the birdhouses—this will give you a very powerful marketing tool (environmentally friendly), as well as keep costs to a minimum, because in most cases used wood can be acquired for free or very cheap. Displaying samples of all of the birdhouses you make and sell at your home (with mom and dad's permission) along with bold attention-grabbing signage will help to draw people and motorists passing by to stop in and browse through your birdhouse selection. In addition to selling from home, birdhouses can also be sold on eBay and internet malls, as well as at weekend flea markets, home and garden shows, and crafts shows. There are a number of web sites where birdhouse construction plans can be bought, including Scrollsaw located online at *d* www.scrollsaw.com, and U-Bild *d* www.u-bild.com.

Handmade Toys

Rocking toys, wooden toys, dolls, dollhouses and accessories, toy boxes, educational toys, die cast toys, antique toy replicas such as pedal cars and pull toys, wooden building blocks, and puzzles are just a few examples of the various handcrafted toys that you can make and sell for big profits. Not only is making and selling handmade toys potentially very profitable, but it can also be a lot of fun, and you will be creating cherished memories for children for years to come. In fact, handcrafted toys often become treasured family heirlooms passed down to each new generation of children to enjoy. Fortunately, you do not need much in the way of special skills or equipment to start making and selling handmade high-quality toys. You will need a small workshop space outfitted with basic tools (and the help of an adult if you are inexperienced using woodworking tools), and toy design and construction plans, which are widely available from a number of sources online, including Wooden Toy Plans, ♂ www.woodentoyplans.com, and U-Bild ♂ www.u-bild.com. The Doll Net located online at ♂ www.thedoll net.com, also provides an excellent source of information about doll making and supplies. Because handcrafted toys of all types are always in high-demand, they can be sold many ways, including selling online using eBay and internet malls, and in the bricks-and-mortar world by renting table space at craft shows, toys shows, and flea markets.

Fashion Design

What does it take for young people to break into the world of fashion design? Great designs, a determination to succeed, and persistence to ensure you do succeed. To get started there are basically three routes you can choose. One, you can design and manufacture fashion clothing and sell to department stores or chain fashion retailers. Two, you can design and manufacture fashion clothing and sell to small independent fashion boutiques. Three, you can design and manufacture fashion clothing for private clients. Each option has advantages and disadvantages, but all three share a common thread (no pun intended): great fashions start with great designs. Initially, concentrate on creating sketches of the clothing you want to make. Pick a few of your best designs and make sample garments, which can be shown to fashion buyers. If you do not sew at the level needed for fashion clothing, you will need to contract with a local seamstress to initially sew the garments. You will want to specialize in specific fashion styles, such as casual, sports, or work fashions, aimed at a specific target audience, such as children, teens, young adults, professionals, or seniors. And don't forget to get friends and family wearing your fashion designs, because this is a great way to get your fashions out there and people talking. Fashion Schools Online is a directory of schools offering fashion design classes, which can be found on the web at ♂ www.fashion schools.com. The National Association of Fashion and Accessory Designers located online at ♂ www.nafad.com, is also a good starting point for gaining additional information about the fashion design industry.

Hand-Painted Storage Boxes

People are always looking for unique ways to organize and store their personal items, kitchenware, and business documents, which is why one-of-a-kind hand-painted storage boxes have become big sellers. Using materials such as wood, metal, plastic, fabric, cardboard, or a combination of these, you can design and build simple storage boxes and paint them to suit every décor or storage application. Woodworkers Workshop, located online at ♂ www.freewoodworking plans.com, and Wood Zone, located online at ♂ www.woodzone.com, both sell easy to use storage box construction plans. Painted images can depict landscapes, abstract designs, animals, or let your customers choose the types of images they want painted on the storage boxes. Don't worry if you lack artistic skills, you can concentrate on building and selling the storage boxes and hire an artist (perhaps a friend) to do the artistic painting. Or if the artistic part is your thing, you can hunt flea markets and secondhand stores for potential wood-storage items that you can paint and fix up. There are numerous options for selling the finished products including online sales, on a wholesale basis to retailers, exhibiting at home décor and gift shows, direct to interior designers and professional organizers, and by renting sales space on weekends at public markets, mall kiosks, and flea markets.

Funky Fashion Accessories

Perhaps you are more interested in designing and making fashion accessories than fashion clothing. The same holds true for designing and making fashion accessories: If you have a flair for design, then why not break into the fashion accessories designers' industry? It is not as difficult as you might think. Get started by picking a fashion accessory to design, produce, and sell. It could be just about anything, including bridal veils, handbags, shoes, belts, belt buckles, costume jewelry, wraps, wallets, or even vintage reproductions of top designers like Fendi, Gucci, and Prada. The options for selling fashion accessories are also numerous. You can sell to family, friends, and neighbors, sell your fashion accessories online utilizing eBay and internet malls, or rent booth space at consumer fashion shows and mall kiosks.

Or, if you're a big thinker (and you should be!), you can sell your fashion accessory products wholesale to fashion accessory retailers. There are many books available on the topic of designing and creating fashion accessories such as 📖 *Making Handbags: Retro, Chic, Luxurious* by Ellen Goldstein-Lynch, Sarah Mullins, and Nicole Malone (Rockport Publishers, 2002). A good place to search for these types of books is through Amazon at ✆ www.amazon.com. The National Association of Fashion and Accessory Designers, located online at ✆ www.nafad.com, also provides many helpful links and resources.

T-Shirt Printing

Silk-screening and selling T-shirts can earn you big bucks. How much profit? Lots of extra money, especially when you consider that you can buy T-shirts in bulk for as little as $2 each wholesale, spend another 50 cents on the silk-screening process, and retail each shirt for up to $20. That's a whopping $17.50 gross profit on every sale! Other products and garments that can be silk-screened for profit include mouse pads, sweaters, sports bags, hats, and aprons. In total you will have to invest about $10,000 into equipment and supplies to get started, unless you buy used silk-screening equipment, then you can cut your start up costs to about $5,000. The equipment is relatively small and can easily be set up in a garage or in the basement. This is not a cheap business to start, but the potential profits can easily pay your way through college, or if you really like the business, you can turn it into a full-time enterprise after you graduate. You can sell your screen-printed T-shirts direct to consumers at flea markets, sports and recreation shows, concerts, community events, eBay and other online marketplaces, and by renting kiosk space at malls and at the beach on weekends and during holidays. You can also sell silk-screened clothing to corporations, clubs, and sports teams. Atlas Screen Supply sells silk screening equipment and supplies. They can be contacted at ☎ (800) 621-4173, or online at ✆ www.atlasscreensupply.com. Silkscreen Biz, located online at ✆ www.silkscreen.biz, also sells screen printing equipment and supplies.

Artistic Ability

If you have the artistic ability to create beautiful works of art, then why not share this gift with the world and make lots of extra cash in the process? Regardless of the medium—oil or watercolor paintings, ink drawings, sculptures in stone, wood, or iron—creating and selling fine art or folk art can be a very profitable way to earn extra cash. The hard work is producing the art; the easy work is selling it because people love art. In the virtual art world you can develop your own web site to sell your works of art, sell through eBay, or sell through any number of the online virtual art galleries, such as Folk Art Marketplace located at ♂ www.folk-art .com. In the bricks-and-mortar world you can sell your art through established art galleries, through art auction sales, from home, and by exhibiting your work at art shows, home décor shows, and renting mall kiosk space on weekends, especially leading up to Christmas. Also contact interior designers and give them first viewing and the first opportunity to purchase your art for their clients on a semi-exclusive basis. In fact, you should combine all of these selling methods along with accepting commissioned assignments to ensure maximum exposure and maximum profitability.

Christmas Decorations

Did you know that consumers from around the globe spend millions on hand-crafted Christmas decorations every year? Cashing in on the demand is easier than most young people think. Forget about making and selling mass-produced decorations; the marketplace is already flooded with cheap, low quality Christmas decorations. Instead concentrate on making and selling high-quality hand-made decorations that over time will become cherished family heirlooms. Wreaths, table centers, tree ornaments, tree toppers, and monogrammed mantel stockings are all popular with consumers. Supplies to make decorations are available at crafts supply wholesalers, and many of the raw materials such as pinecones and cedar greens can be obtained for free just by going for a walk in the woods. Practice makes perfect, so you should work on your creations long before the October to December prime selling season. Constantly look for ways to make your current designs better as well as creating new products. Books such as 📖 *Christmas Ornaments to Make* (Better Homes and Gardens, 2002) and 📖 *Wreaths for Every Season* by June Apel and Chalice Bruce (North Light Books, 2002) are great resources and full of lots of helpful tips and diagrams to help you get started making your own decorations. Sell your custom Christmas decoration creations direct to consumers at Christmas craft shows and by renting mall kiosks and vending cart space leading up to Christmas. You can also sell your products online using eBay and marketplaces specific to Christmas, such as the Christmas Mall located at ♂ www.christmasmall.us. Additional sales options include consignment sales through gift retailers in your community, as well as selling wholesale to independent and chain gift retailers.

Models

There are a couple ways that you can earn extra cash making and selling models. One, you can design and construct handcrafted models. Two, you can purchase model kits and assemble and sell them. If you choose the first option and hand-craft models from wood, stone, metal, ceramic, die cast, fabric, or injection plastic, considerably more artistic skills and equipment will be needed than are needed to assemble models from kits. If you choose to assemble models from kits, the most popular kinds of models include boats, sailing ships, automobiles, trains, air-planes, and military machinery, all of which can be purchased at wholesale prices from model manufacturers or distributors. Harness the power of the internet to find a reliable source. Unlike designing and building handcrafted models, assem-bling model kits only requires basic modelers' tools, a workbench, and good light-ing, and all of these items are available at most hobby and craft shops. Once completed, handcrafted models and models assembled from kits can be mounted on a display base or under glass to increase the value. The best ways to sell mod-els is through online marketplaces such as eBay and by renting table space on weekends at craft and hobby shows.

Art Jewelry

Calling all creative young entrepreneurs! It is time to earn a ton of extra cash by making and selling beautiful art jewelry. Art jewelry is a catch phrase covering all nonprecious stone jewelry. Art jewelry can be created from many kinds of raw mate-rials individually or in combination, including metals, plastics, stones, ceramics, fabrics, bone and shell, and exotic hardwoods and softwoods. And you can even incorporate some precious stones and materials such as silver and turquoise into your designs. The basic skills and knowledge that you will need to learn can include mold making, casting, soldering, polishing, gem and stone cutting, and setting. But don't worry because there are art jewelry classes taught in every small town and big city across the nation. There are also a multitude of books and videos available on the subject of art jewelry making, and with practice, the learning curve is short. Once you are up to speed and producing art jewelry, it can be sold to or consigned with fashion, jewelry, and gift retailers, as well as art galleries, or sold wholesale to retailers at discounted prices. You can also sell to friends and family, and at table space on weekends at flea markets, craft shows, and mall kiosks, as well as selling online through eBay and internet malls. Art jewelry making equipment and sup-plies are easy to find online through companies such as Auntie's Beads ♂ www .auntiesbeads.com, and the Jewelry Supply ♂ www.jewelrysupplies.com.

Woodcraft Products

Providing you have basic woodworking skills and dad or mom will let you use the family workshop and tools, you have the potential to earn excellent part-time profits making and selling simple woodcraft products. The best woodcraft products to make include clock cases, picture frames, storage boxes, toy boxes, lamp bases, woodturning bowls and spindles, masks, canoe paddles, furniture components, and whirligigs and lawn ornaments. Design and construction plans for these woodcraft products and many more are readily available through a number of online sources such as U-Bild ♂ www.u-bild.com and Scrollsaw ♂ www.scrollsaw.com. If you are creative, you can design your own woodcraft products. In addition to making products from rare and exotic woods, also try to incorporate recycled wood. Doing so will give you a very powerful marketing tool (environmentally friendly), as well as it helps to keep material costs to a minimum as in most cases used wood can be acquired for free. Woodcrafts can be sold online through a number of electronic marketplaces such as eBay ♂ www.ebay.com, the Craft Mall ♂ www.craftmall.com, as well as by renting table space at flea markets, crafts shows, and church bazaars, especially leading up to Christmas.

Piñatas

Making and selling party piñatas is a great way for young entrepreneurs to earn extra cash, not to mention they are also very easy to make, and just as easy to sell because piñatas are always in demand. Piñatas aren't just for kid's birthday parties any more. Working from the kitchen table you can make and sell piñatas for just about any type of party or special event, including anniversary parties, weddings, graduations, adult birthdays, special achievement celebrations, Christmas piñatas and other holidays, baby showers, and lots more. Newspaper, craft paper, paint, glue, water, and any type of bead embellishments are all you need to get started. The difference among piñatas is how they are designed and what prizes are hidden inside; the prizes and piñatas match the theme of the event and the people attending. As mentioned, piñatas are also easy to sell. You can sell direct to friends, family, and neighbors hosting special events, as well as selling completed piñatas online through eBay and internet malls, and direct to restaurants and day-care centers. Be sure to build alliances with wedding and event planners that regularly organize birthdays and other celebrations, as they can become a very good source for repeat business. If you are really ambitious, you can even sell piñatas to retailers on a wholesale basis.

Kites

About $100 is all that is needed to cover the costs of construction materials and basic marketing materials, such as fliers, signs, and business cards to start designing selling handcrafted kites. Don't worry if you have never built a kite before, because there is lots of information online about kite design and construction. A good starting point is the American Kite Fliers Association web site located at ♂ www.aka.kite.org. There are also many books devoted to the subject of kite design and construction, such as ▭ *The Kite Making Handbook* by Rosella Guerra and Giuseppe Ferlengna (David & Charles Publishers, 2004). Once you have mastered building kites through trial-and-error and practice, a great low-cost sales tactic to use is to host try-before-you-buy kite-flying events. Setup at a local park, beach, or parking lot (with permission) and let potential customers fly kites of their choice before committing to buying. Advertise the event by informing the local media in the form of a press release. When creating the press release, emphasize family fun. Given the unique aspect of the event, there should be no problem in securing lots of free and valuable media exposure. Kites are so visual that on the day of the event it will not take long until a crowd assembles to see what is going on, and soon people will be lining up to fly and buy your kites. In addition to try-before-you-buy kite sales events, you can also sell your kites online through eBay and internet malls, and by renting vendor space on weekends at sports and recreation shows, flea markets, and public markets.

Tie-Dyed Clothing

Funky tie-dyed clothing is back in vogue and you can make a bundle of loot making and selling your own tie-dye designs. As the name suggests, creating tie-dye clothing is the process of tieing clothing using elastics or folds and rinsing the garment in one or more clothing dye solutions to create permanent colorful patterns on the clothing. There are three basic tieing techniques used to create the design: spirals, accordion folds, and sunburst. All are easily learned with practice, which means every kid, teen, and young adult is qualified to make and sell tie-dyed clothing. The most popular garments to tie-dye and sell include T-shirts, sun hats, cotton pants, and beach shorts and wraps, although just about any type of garment can be tie-dyed, especially ones made of cotton fabrics. Clothing blanks, dyes, and a laundry tub for dye washing and rinsing are about all you need to get started. Tie-dye clothing can be sold to friends and family, and in other various ways including through internet malls, and on weekends by renting booth space at flea markets, music concerts, sporting events, and at community events like fairs and parades. There are numerous companies selling tie-dye supplies, such as G.S. Dye, ☎ (800) 596-05550, ♂ www.gsdye.com, Jacquard Products, ☎ (800) 442-0455, ♂ www.jacquardproducts.com, and The Standard Dyes Company, ☎ (800) 859-1240, ♂ www.standarddyes.com.

Twig Furniture and Crafts

Have fun and earn extra money on weekends and during summer holidays by making and selling twig furniture, twig garden products, and twig crafts. Outdoor furniture, birdhouses, tables, chairs, bentwood arbors, trellis, planters, mirror frames, picture frames, and lots more, can all be easily made from willow and birch twigs and branches. The learning curve is quick, and a walk through the woods collecting branches (with permission) will supply you with all the raw materials you need to get going. 📖 *Making Twig Furniture and Household Things* by Abby Rouff (Hartley & Marks Publishers, 1999), is a great source of information to get you started. The Twig Factory, found online at ♂ www.twig factory.com, also provides information about building twig furniture and crafts, and they sell design plans for various twig furniture and craft products. Fortunately, not much money is needed to start because the required tools and fasteners add up to nothing more than basic hand tools, a power saw, and a drill press, along with carpenter's glue, wire, and screws to assemble twig creations. You can sell finished products online through eBay at ♂ www.ebay.com, and The Crafters Mall, ♂ www.procrafter.com, as well as to friends, family, and neighbors, and by renting booth space at flea markets, craft shows, and garden shows on weekends.

Trinket Boxes

Trinket boxes are great for storing jewelry, coins, keys, and keepsakes, and lots more. Trinket boxes are also very easy to make, even if you have limited craft and artist abilities, which makes them terrific items for just about anyone to build and sell for a profit. There are a number of companies selling easy-to-use trinket box construction plans; a few of these include, U-Bild ♂ www.u-bild .com, Wood Projects ♂ www.woodprojects.com, and Wood Zone ♂ www.wood zone.com. Use interesting materials, such as exotic wood, copper, glass, shells, beads, ceramic tiles, and mirrors to make your boxes unique. Selling trinket boxes is just as easy as making them, mainly because you can keep prices low and they make excellent gifts for birthdays, weddings, Christmas, and anniversaries. Sell them at craft shows, flea markets, and online via eBay and internet malls. Also make a few sample boxes and visit jewelry shops and gift retailers and inquire about placing them in these shops on consignment, or even better, offer them to retailers at wholesale pricing and sell them in bulk.

Handmade Paper

Papermaking is a little known business opportunity that can generate exceptional profits. What I really like about this enterprise is that there are two revenue sources: making custom paper from scratch or producing and selling papermaking craft products. Both are relatively easy to learn using training aids such as papermaking classes, books, and videos. Handmade paper is used in papermaking craft products as well as by artisans producing specialty gift cards, place cards, note cards, birthday cards, gift tags, wedding invitations, birth announcements, wrapping paper, watermarked stationery, watercolor paintings, matting art, pressed flower art, and calligraphy. A few of the handcrafted papermaking products you can produce include mobiles, lampshades, paper lanterns, paper window shades, and paper jewelry. Handmade paper can be sold directly to artisans, while papermaking craft products can be sold to gift retailers wholesale, or directly to consumers utilizing online venues such as eBay and internet craft malls, or by exhibiting products at craft fairs. Helpful papermaking craft web sites include Hand Papermaking, ♂ www.handpapermaking.org, International Association of Hand Papermakers and Paper Artists, ♂ www.iapma.info, and Paper Making, ♂ www.papermaking.net, all of which provide useful industry information and resources.

Decorative Glass Products

There are a few techniques that can be used to etch decorative glass—acid wash, engraving, laser etching, and sandblasting. Sandblasting remains the most popular choice; you cover the glass with a stencil pattern and blow sand against the surface and the area not protected by the pattern becomes etched. Glass etching is a great moneymaking opportunity for many reasons, but mainly because it is quick to learn, equipment and supplies are very inexpensive, you can work from a garage workshop, and demand for decorative etched glass is high. Reading books such as 📖 *Easy Glass Etching* by Marlis Cornett (Sterling, 2004), will help you shorten the glass etching learning curve, and companies like Martronics Corporation, ☎ (800) 775-0797, ♂ www.glass-etching-kits.com, sell glass etching tools and supplies. You also will need some basic safety equipment such as safety glasses. Products that can be etched with eloquent designs, patterns, and images for resale include window glass, cabinet glass, glass awards, glass tables, signs on door and window glass, automotive glass, mirrors, glassware, and sun catchers, as well as etching glass with codes and identification marks for security purposes. You can buy ready-made etching stencil designs and letter stencils or make your own. In addition to selling etched glass products online and at home décor shows, you can also do custom one-of-a-kind glass etching work for interior designers, kitchen cabinet installers, and automotive dealers.

Essential Oils

Essential oils are extracted from aromatic plants by steam, distillation or expression extraction. Essential oils can be applied topically or inhaled, and act on physical, emotional, and psychological processes. They can be used as fragrant ingredients in a wide variety of health and beauty products, including cosmetics, body lotions, soaps, candles, aromatherapy burners, perfume, and aromatic potpourri products. There are basically two ways to extract essential oils from herbs and flowers—distillation and expression. Distillation is the most common method and involves using steam to break down plant tissue, causing it to release essential oil in a vaporized form. The vapors travel from the distillation chamber into cooling tanks, causing the vapors to become liquid, which is then separated from the water leaving pure essential oil. You can make your own essential oil distiller, although I recommend purchasing a commercial distiller, which will set you back about $1,000. The Essential Oil Company, ✆ www.essentialoil.com, sells professional distillation equipment.

The expression, or cold pressing extraction method involves mixing the plants with citrus oils and pressing the mixture, the resulting liquid is then filtered to separate the pure essential oils, but this method yields much less essential oil than distillation based on plant volume. The retail-selling price of essential oils is directly related to how much plant material is needed for distillation as well as the cost of the plants. The more plants that are needed and the cost of these plants translates into higher manufacturing costs, which must be recouped with higher selling prices. Essential oils can be sold in bulk to companies manufacturing and selling health and beauty products, or sold directly to consumers online, at craft fairs, and mail order sales. Reading books like 📖 *The Complete Book of Essential Oils and Aromatherapy* by Valerie Ann Worwood (New World Library, 1991), is a great source for learning more about making essential oils.

CHAPTER

6

SPORTS AND RECREATIONAL OPPORTUNITIES

Calling all young sports and recreation enthusiasts! In this chapter you will discover lots of excellent moneymaking opportunities in sports and recreation. You can earn extra cash with your own beach equipment rental business. Or perhaps raising and selling fishing bait is more up your alley. And, if you are a true fitness guru, you might even start a personal fitness trainer business. The best aspect about working in sports and recreation, is that more times than not, you will be able to do what you already enjoy, and get paid for it!

Tour Guide

Galleries, museums, amusement parks, ski resorts, and hotels commonly hire or contract with independent tour guides to explain attractions and acquaint customers with onsite amenities, as well as local attractions. Whether you contract with a local business or start an independent community tour guide service, the business can be inexpensively started and there is an excellent opportunity to earn great money working flexible hours. If you choose the independent route, then in addition to the usual tour stops at the oldest and most architecturally interesting buildings, the best beaches, a pedicab ride through the park, and area museums, also show off a little bit of the more unusual sights of your community—crime scenes, movie or television set locations, and past or present celebrity houses. Personal tour guides charge $150 to $200 for half-day tours, and up to $350 for full-day tours plus the cost of transportation and tickets to events and attractions. Providing clients with an unforgettably fun experience combined with incredible service gives you the two main ingredients needed to secure referral and repeat business. Promote the service aggressively by building alliances with businesses and individuals such as coach and taxi drivers, event planners, hotels, restaurants, and travel agents so they can refer your personally guided tours to their clients. Likewise, be sure to also market your services to corporations that want to treat their visiting out-of-town customers, employees, and executives to a special event. The National Federation of Tourist Guide Associations in the United States, located online at ♂ www.nftga.com, provides information and resources, as does the Canadian Tour Guide Association, located online at ♂ www.ctgaoftoronto.org.

Fishing Bait

Fishing bait is big business in North America and you can earn serious extra money selling all kinds of bait, although you will need to be comfortable handling creepy crawly things like worms, leaches, and minnows. Bait minnows, like shiners, can be caught in rivers and creeks using traps or a seine net. A license issued by the Department of Fisheries is generally required to catch fishing bait minnows, so be sure to check regulations in your area before getting started. Dew worms are another popular bait, which can be raised in soil or moss boxes in a dark area, or you can pick worms at golf courses and parks after sunset, especially after a rain. In terms of selling fishing bait, you have a few options. The first is to sell right from home providing mom and dad don't mind. The second option is to go to locations where people fish (lakes, rives, and streams) and sell direct. The third option is to contact bait shops or country stores in your area and offer to sell your bait at wholesale pricing. Shield Publications publishes books on raising bait for profit. They can be found online at ♂ www.wormbooks.com. The Bait Net is also a good source of industry information and links and they can be found online ♂ www.baitnet.com.

Fishing Tackle

For all of the young entrepreneurial fishing enthusiasts out there, great profits can be earned buying low-cost fishing tackle and equipment and reselling it to fishing fanatics for huge profits. Best-selling products include rods, reels, lures, knives, fish finder electronics, waders, clipper tools, traps, line, subject books, float tubes, vests, tackle boxes, downriggers, and electric trolling motors. The best buying sources are wholesalers and direct from manufacturers, while the best selling sources include eBay, fishing and hunting shows, flea markets, and mail order sales. If you can afford to buy in volume, you will get the lowest prices purchasing factory direct from overseas manufacturers, especially in China, which has a large fishing tackle manufacturing industry. Also do not overlook local fly tiers as a possible buying source for one-of-a-kind-ties, as these can easily be sold for two or three times cost and sell like crazy. One of the best ways to spread the word is to get out to the rivers and lakes in your area and let people fishing know about the products you sell. There are a number of fishing tackle wholesalers and manufacturers such as Dollar Days Wholesale, ♂ www.dollardays.com, Pokee Fishing Tackle, ♂ www.pokeefishing.com, and Valor, ♂ www.valorcorp.com.

Fitness Equipment

Buying and selling secondhand fitness equipment is an excellent way for young people to earn a ton of extra cash. There is always great supply of all types of hardly used fitness equipment because many people who purchase new fitness equipment soon discover that working out every day is hard work and very time consuming. And in no time the very expensive piece of exercise equipment becomes a very expensive clothes rack. Pick up any buy-and-sell type newspaper, and you will find many ads that read something like, "Treadmill used only ten times paid $2,500, sell $750 OBO." Even though excellent quality equipment can be purchased cheaply, that does not mean you cannot resell it for huge profits; you can. Remember, much of sales is simply timing, and in the case of fitness equipment, it does not take long before someone else will come along and want to get fit. As mentioned, fitness equipment can be purchased through classified ads, but also at garage sales, gym closeouts, auctions, and estate sales. Best sellers include treadmills, steppers, elliptical trainers, rowing machines, exercise bikes, free weights, and universal multi-station machines. You can sell the equipment from home and advertise locally in the paper and on community bulletin boards, and you can also list your equipment for sale on any number of online marketplaces.

Golf Ball Printing

Golf ball printing is a terrific moneymaking opportunity for just about any teen or young adult. All you need to get started in the multimillion dollar personalized golf ball industry is to purchase golf balls in bulk at wholesale prices, and a simple pad printer. The rest is pretty easy: Market the business, take orders, print golf balls, and you're on your way to earning extra cash. For those not familiar with personalized golf balls, they are nothing more than common golf balls that are printed with a person's name, a business name and logo, or the name of an organization, depending on the customer. Personalized golf balls make fantastic gifts for the golf fanatic, as well as for businesses of all sizes to give to clients as an appreciation gift and at golf tournaments. The low-mess and zero noise aspects of the printing equipment means you only need minimal working space, and with your parents' permission you can set up in a spare bedroom, garage, or in the basement. Finding customers is not difficult because America is golf crazy and golfers love to have his or her name boldly printed on their golf balls. Advertise locally in the newspaper, take online orders for mail-order shipping, exhibit at golf and recreation shows, and sell through golf retailers, pro shops, and golf courses on a revenue-share program. Also don't forget to start selling to family, friends, and neighbors. Landing business and corporate customers is as easy as calling and explaining why you are the right candidate to supply printed golf balls for their next company golf tournament. There are a number of companies selling golf ball printing equipment and supplies online, including KingBo Golf, ♂ www.kingbo-golf.com, Printex USA, ♂ www.printexusa.com, and Winon USA, ♂ www.win onusa.com.

Little League Trading Cards

There are literally thousands of little league teams playing in all the common sports and more across the North America. How can you earn part-time profits from these amateur sports teams? Easy—produce and sell little league team photograph and statistic trading cards just like the professional trading cards, complete with the player's photograph and name on the front and team statistics on the back. The investment needed to start this type of business venture adds up to little more than the cost of a digital camera, computer, desktop publishing software, and marketing supplies. You can contract with a local print shop to print the cards once you have secured orders. The trading cards can be sold to players and parents, or you can opt not to charge the players or their parents for the cards, but to charge the current team sponsor or new sponsor in exchange for having its business name emblazoned across the front and back of the trading card. For young entrepreneurs seeking a fun and potentially very profitable moneymaking opportunity, this just may be what you have been looking for.

Bicycle Repair

Mechanically-inclined young people with a love for cycling can earn excellent cash repairing bicycles right from a simple home workshop. There are many advantages to starting a bicycle repair service, including low costs to operate, huge demand for the service in an ever-growing sport, and you can work flexible part-time hours nights and weekends, or whatever suits your school timetable. Even if you are not experienced in bicycle repairs, there are a number of schools offering bicycle mechanic courses that take only a few weeks to complete, such as those offered by United Bicycle Institute in Oregon, located online at ♂ www.bike school.com, as well as courses offered by Barnett Bicycle Institute, ♂ www.bbin stitute.com. Market your bicycle repair services to friends and family as well as cycling enthusiasts in your community by pinning promotional fliers to bulletin boards and running low-cost classified ads in your local newspaper. Describe your services, give contact telephone number, and include an introductory offer, such as a seasonal bicycle tune-up at a very low cost to attract new business. When you are not busy repairing your own customers' bikes, you can also work for bicycle retailers to handle their overflow repair and warranty work.

Fitness Trainer

If you love and practice fitness training, then you should know that the time has never been better than right now to start your own personal fitness-trainer business, teaching people from five to ninety five how to live a more healthy life through the implementation and maintenance of exercise programs. Your target audience will include any person who wants to become more fit. You can work one-on-one with anyone and everyone interested in increasing their level of fitness, or specialize and train busy executives, kids, disabled persons, moms-to-be, or seniors at their offices or homes. Right now there are currently no across-the-board certification requirements to become a personal trainer. However, if you find that being a fitness trainer is something that you enjoy and might want to pursue after you have finished school, then I would urge you to take professional training to become certified. You can contact the International Fitness Professionals Association by telephone at ☎ (800) 785-1924, or online at ♂ www.ifpa-fitness .com, for more information about certification programs offered in your area. Or, contact the National Federation of Professional Trainers by telephone at ☎ (800) 729-6378 or online at ♂ www.nfpt.com to find out more about the certification programs they offer. If fitness training is your ambition, you can open your own fitness studio and offer one-on-one and group training programs to everyone, as well as work in fitness clubs, community centers, retirement homes, hospitals, cruise ships, corporations, hotels, spas, resorts, camps, schools, or with people in their own homes.

Bicycle Touring

Have fun and pedal your way to big profits by starting a bicycle tour business. The key to success is to create unique, fun, and interesting tours for your customers. You might want to focus on a central theme, such as tours through an historic part of the city, or leisurely rides through the countryside, or for the more adventurous, mountain biking in the woods on steep terrain. So what do you need to get started? You need a keen interest in cycling, durable bicycles suited to the type of tours, a few helmets, basic first-aid training and a first-aid kit, and a marketing strategy to lure in customers. In total, expect to invest a few thousand dollars. One idea to kick things into high gear from the get-go might be to start in partnership with an existing tour operator or tourist-related business that does not currently provide bicycle tour options to clients. Or, you can simply start new and market the tours through local travel agents, the chamber of commerce, and community travel and recreation agencies. Current rates for bicycle tours range from $60 per person for half-day excursions, to $100 for full day, to as much as $2,500 for week-long trips. However, I would suggest that you start small and offer half- and full-day tours and provide a light lunch and snacks.

Golf Caddy

If you can carry a golf bag for eighteen holes of golf, then you are qualified to make lots of extra cash working as a freelance golf caddy. Caddy rates vary by experience. Of course, professional caddies can earn upwards of a six-figure annual income, but their duties are vastly different then what yours will be. Professional caddies help to read the course and select clubs; your duties are basically to carry the bag, fix divits, and retrieve out-of-play balls. So expect to earn in the range of $15 to $25 per round, plus a gratuity. So who can you caddy for? Start by offering your services to family and friends and branch out from there. You will be surprised by how many weekend golfers are prepared to part with a few bucks to have a caddy, and news always travels fast on any golf course. Therefore, once you have a few caddy gigs under your belt, it won't take long until other golfers are asking if you're available to caddy.

Mobile Mini Golf Business

Miniature golf is extremely popular, and you can capitalize on this popularity and profit by starting a mobile mini golf business. Providing you have a creative flair and handyperson skills, you can easily design and build a mini golf course using materials like plywood and outdoor carpet or turf, and even design the course around a central theme, such as a pirate ship, space, or fairytale story. The advantages of making the course in sections is so that it can easily be packed-up and moved using a truck or trailer, so you will have the ability to set up the miniature golf course in high-traffic tourist areas, such as at the beach or grocery store parking lot, or rent out the entire course for special events such as birthday parties and corporate events. Also, you don't have to own or rent land to create the course. Even though the initial start-up costs are substantial, in the range of $25,000 or more, the profit potential is excellent as you can charge $5 per person to play, and rent out the course for as much as $300 per day for events.

Pedal Boat Rental

Did you know that a small fleet of just ten pedal boats can generate as much as $30,000 in rental revenue in a single three-month season? And what's even more exciting is that one person can easily operate this business. To establish a pedal boat rental business you will need a waterfront location to operate from, either a calm river or lake. The location can be independent or in partnership with an existing business such as a marina, waterfront park, or campground. The business can be supported by walk-in traffic, as well as two-for-one coupons that can be distributed to tourists and locals for use during slower mid-week periods. Extra income can be earned by adding a small catering cart that sells soft drinks, candy bars, and popcorn. You will need to invest in your boats and related equipment such as life vests and safety equipment. Currently pedal boats can be purchased for about $1,000 each. In total expect to invest in the range of $15,000 plus the cost of any lease improvements such as painting or repairing the docks. While the investment is higher than most of the moneymaking ventures listed in the book, the return on investment can be in just a month or two, not to mention that you will also realized be working in a very relaxing environment.

Paintball

If you have ever participated in a paintball game, you know what it's like. Paintball games places you in direct competition with family and friends, and teams are formed using paintball guns to shoot paintballs at each other in a strategic game of war or cat and mouse. Market the business by going directly to large groups of people who will use a day of paintball war games as an opportunity to take part in an event that can include a large portion of their entire group. Ideal candidates are corporations, schools, clubs, and sports associations. The main requirement for this business venture is land to operate and host the paintball game events, but with a little effort it may be possible to negotiate a profit-split arrangement with the owner of the land where the games will be played. An enclosed trailer or shed should also be located on the event site to serve as a portable office and for equipment storage. You will also need a portable toilet on site; these can be easily rented by the month. Secondary requirements include liability insurance, first-aid equipment, and emergency action plans. You can charge each player in the range of $50 to $75 including equipment rental and paintballs. Even operating weekends only, a paintball games business can easily generate profits in the range of $20,000 to $30,000 per year. Badlands Paintball Wholesale, ♂ www.badlandspaintball.com, and National Paintball Supply, ♂ www.nationalpaintball.com, both sell paintball equipment and supplies at discounted wholesale prices.

7

ONLINE AND COMPUTER BUSINESSES

There are almost an unlimited number ways that you can earn big bucks with computers either by selling products/ services online to consumers around the globe or by starting and operating a computer-related business. In fact, there are so many options that volumes could be written on the topic. Since this book covers many different ways that young people can earn extra money, I have limited this chapter to include only the best ways to make money online and with computers, such as starting a web design service, a computer repair service, an eBay business, and by offering clients a wide variety of desktop publishing services.

Web Designer

Tech-savvy young entrepreneurs can cash in on the boom in web design services. How? With thousands of new web sites and web pages posted to the internet every day, web design is in great demand. But competition in web design is steep. You might want to take a more grassroots approach to marketing and start by servicing your local area, at least in the beginning while you build a reputation. Beyond working your own current connections (friends, family, and their referrals), get started by designing a few sample web sites and pages to showcase your design talents. Be sure to mix up your sample work to include an e-commerce site, an information portal, a blog, and so on. Next, initiate a direct marketing campaign using introduction and sales letters, telephone calls, and email blasts, along with personal visits to introduce your web design services to small business owners in your community that currently do not have a business web site, or that have a site in need of improvement. Armed with a notebook computer you can meet with business owners, present your sample sites, and explain the benefits of your web design services. You can earn extra money by offering additional services such as web site hosting, maintaining and updating sites, and providing content and web tools. The Web Design Developers Association located online at ♂ www .wdda.org, provides lots of helpful information and resources.

Electronic Magazine

Thanks to the advent of the internet, publishing your own e-zine (electronic magazine) is easy. In spite of the estimated 100,000 daily, weekly, and monthly electronic publications being distributed to millions of online readers, there is always room for a new one. Develop your e-zine based on what you know and like—sports, music, movies, or just about anything else that tickles your informative fancy. Include stories, pictures, contests, and surveys related to the theme of the magazine. You can research and write content yourself, as well as accepting readers' submissions and buying low-cost content from online providers. Most e-zines are typically free to subscribers and supported by selling advertising, which means businesses rent space in your electronic magazine to advertise their products and services. For instance, if you publish and distribute a monthly skateboard e-zine, then logical advertisers would include skateboard manufacturers and retailers. To stand out in the marketplace, aim to serve a well-defined niche market, provide interesting and informative content that readers cannot get anywhere else, and build a large subscription base that will appeal to advertisers and marketers that want to reach your readership base. Ezine Director located at ♂ www.ezinedirector.com, sells e-zine delivery and management software, and the Ezine Directory lists over 2,400 electronic publications. The web site is located at ♂ www.ezine-dir.com.

Online Research

If you find yourself spending a lot of time surfing the web, and you want to make some extra cash, consider starting an internet research service so you can get paid for the time you spend surfing. Not long ago this business opportunity was referred to as information brokering, but, with the introduction of the internet, the name has changed. The business remains the same, however, as the information that was once researched and compiled from newspapers, trade magazines, and business and industry journals can now be found on online. An internet research service operates in two ways. First, researchers collect data and facts relevant to a specific topic or topics and then sell the compiled data to individuals and businesses. Second, business owners and marketers often hire an internet researcher to search for specific data and facts relevant to their particular businesses, industries, or markets. Either way, clients pay for information they are seeking. The amount of money you can charge varies depending on how much research time is required to compile the data and related costs, but expect to charge in the area of $25 to $35 per hour. More information about internet researching can be found online at the Association of Internet Researchers, ♂ www.aoir.org. Additionally, a helpful book on the subject is 📖 *Building & Running a Successful Research Business: A Guide for the Independent Information Professional* by Mary Ellen Bates (Cyberage Books, 2003).

Computer Repair

Capitalize on your knowledge of computers and cash in on the multibillion-dollar computer industry by starting your own computer repair service. You can repair computers nights, weekends, and during the holidays from a small homebased workspace, or on a mobile basis if you have access to transportation. Of course, you can also combine both methods to appeal to a wider base of potential customers. In addition to offering computer repair, maintenance, and troubleshooting services, you can also provide customers with computer and related technologies setup, including setting up new computers, installing software, and hooking up printers, monitors, and scanners. Market your services through traditional advertising formats such as running low-cost classified ads in your local newspaper, pinning fliers to bulletin boards, and by creating and implementing a direct-mail campaign aimed mainly at business customers with multiple computer workstations. That way you can offer on-call emergency computer repair services during nonschool hours. Finally the best part: computer repair technicians earn up to $50 per hour, and as the world continues its push toward complete and total computerization, it means that there will always be lots of computers to repair and maintain.

Sell Computers

Selling new and used computers is a great way to earn extra spending cash or put yourself through college. In addition to selling new and used computers, you can also sell computer accessories such as include inkjet printers, laser printers, scanners, DVD and CD writers, LCD monitors, and wireless keyboards and mouse sets, as well as parts including hard drives, memory, audio and video cards, CPUs, and motherboards. New desktop and notebook computer systems, accessories, and parts can be purchased from wholesalers, liquidators, and distributors, and marked up by as much as 50 percent for resale. There are hundreds of reputable companies wholesaling new computers and parts, and the best way to track them down is to conduct a "Google Search" using keyword phrases such as "computer wholesalers." There is also excellent profit potential selling secondhand computer systems, especially notebook computers, which hold their resale value much better than desktop computers. There are companies that even wholesale notebook computers for resale purposes, such as USA Notebooks Used Computer Wholesale ♂ www.usanotebook.com. To buy used computer systems, scan classified ads for bargains and attend auction sales, the preferred method. Many corporations, government agencies, schools, and organization replace their still otherwise good computer equipment on a scheduled basis. These computers can often be purchased for pennies on the dollar of the original cost at auctions or tender sales. The options for selling new and used computer systems, as well as computer accessories are plentiful. You can develop your own web site for sales, sell via eBay and internet malls, or sell direct from home supported by local advertising and word-of-mouth referrals.

Community Web Site Host

Here is a great moneymaking opportunity for young tech-savvy entrepreneurs. Not all small business owners and professionals have the time, ability, or inclination to build, maintain, and regularly update a web site. But at the same time, many would still like to have some sort of presence on the web. Herein lies a great opportunity: Develop, maintain, and market a web site that services a specific neighborhood, town, or city, featuring local news and information, as well as participating businesses and professionals. Each participating business receives space within the site to advertise, promote, and even sell its products and services, along with a web address extension, private email, and a host of additional web and commerce features. You can charge each business a monthly fee that includes fixed services, and additional fees for premium services such as content updating and web tools specific to their businesses. Promote the community web site locally using advertising fliers, coupons, and newspaper ads, as well as getting out and knocking on doors. Offer clients a noncompetition clause to entice them to join. This means one restaurant, one contractor, one lawyer, and so on. The biggest benefit to participating businesses is that they get a fully functioning and regularly updated site for a fraction of what it would cost each individually. Community residents also benefit by getting news and information localized to their specific area along with convenient online access to products and services offered by community businesses. And of course, you benefit by building a successful and profitable part-time business venture.

Run an eBay Business

Can you make big money selling stuff on eBay? Of course you can, just like thousands of other people. In fact, starting your own eBay business is a fantastic way for kids, teens, and young adults to earn a ton of extra cash. The first decision you will need to make is to choose what types of things you are going to sell—new products, used products, or both. Anything can be sold on eBay for big profits. You can sell clothing, electronics, antiques, toys, cookware, collectibles, sporting goods, art, and just about anything else imaginable. If you are going to sell new products, you will need to find a cheap and reliable source. Your options include buying from liquidators, wholesalers, importers, distributors, or directly from manufacturers. Visit your local library or buy a copy of 📖 *202 Things You Can Buy and Sell for Big Profits!* by James Stephenson (Entrepreneur Press, 2004). The book features where and how you can buy more than 200 products for resale. If you are going to sell used products, then a little more work will be needed to acquire and maintain an inventory of saleable merchandise. Depending on the things you plan to sell, used products can be bought cheaply by scouring flea markets, garage sales, auction sales, and estate sales. Collectibles of every sort are always very popular items to sell on eBay. There is a lot to know about eBay and eBay selling, so I strongly suggest that you spend time on eBay sites like the eBay Learning Center, ♂ http://pages.ebay.com/education/index.html, and eBay Seller's Guide, ♂ http://pages.ebay.com/help/sell/index.html/. Also read books like 📖 *Make Big Profits on eBay: Start Your Own Million $ Business* by Jacquelyn Lynn and Charlene Davis (Entrepreneur Press, 2005).

Desktop Publishing Services

The desktop publishing industry is booming, which makes starting a desktop publishing service an excellent moneymaking opportunity for young people with the necessary skills and equipment. Combining your creative design and computer skills, you can provide clients with a wide range of desktop publishing services. With the aid of desktop publishing software programs from Adobe, ♂ www .adobe.com, and Corel, ♂ www.corel.com, you can create electronic promotional fliers, print brochures, product catalogs, business reports, posters, presentations, coupons, and advertisements of all sorts for customers. Best of all, you can work right from home after school and on weekends. Create samples of your work and set appointments with business owners like retail shop owners and cleaning companies and professionals like doctors and lawyers locally to present samples of your work and explain the benefits provided by your service (high-quality, fast, economical, and reliable). You will need to invest in computer equipment, specialized software, a scanner, digital camera, and high quality printer, but with desktop publishing rates in the area of $40 to $100 per hour, you can be assured of a very quick return on investment. Desktop Publishing Online, located at ♂ www.desktoppublishing.com, provides a wealth of information and resources for desktop publishers.

Logo Design Service

If you have a creative flair and artistic abilities, you can put these skills to good use and earn lots of extra cash in the process by designing and selling logos. Great logos help to build and maintain instant brand recognition and consumer awareness by visually linking the logo to the business, product, or service it represents. You will need a computer, digital camera, printer, and design software to get started. Outside of these expenditures, startup costs are minimal and the cost to operate the business is also low—not only can you work from home or your dorm room, but also there are no raw material costs associated with designing and selling logos, just your time. There are two easy ways to get started designing and selling eye-catching logos. The first way is to take a broad approach and simply start designing or redesigning logos for businesses in your community. Once finished, call the business owner to set an appointment to present your work. Close the sale by using the abovementioned persuasions—building brand recognition and consumer awareness. The second option is to design logo samples of fictitious businesses and use these samples to prospect for logo design jobs. You can do this by joining small business groups in your community, such as the chamber of commerce to network for business. In a nutshell, market your logo design talents to business owners and professionals, product developers, non-profit organizations, clubs, government agencies, and to anyone else in need of product, service, or personal branding through repetitive use of logo. The better known you become for your incredible logo designs that perfectly describe what they represent, the higher your fees will go. A helpful book about designing logos is 📖 *Logo Design Workbook: A Hands-On Guide to Creating Logos* by Sean Adams and Noreen Morioka (Rockport Publishers, 2004).

Cartridge Recycling

One of the fastest growing businesses today is ink cartridge recycling. Ink and toner cartridges used in most photocopiers, fax machines, and laser and inkjet printers can easily be recycled simply by replenishing the ink or toner supply, thus keeping them out of the landfill and putting big profits in your pocket! This creates a great environmentally friendly business opportunity for energetic young entrepreneurs to start a toner cartridge recycling business, working from home and on a mobile basis if you have access to transportation. The requirements to start and operate the business are very basic. You will only need simple and inexpensive tools and the ability to refill cartridges with ink, which is easily learned with a little practice. Customers can save as much as 50 percent off the cost of new cartridges by purchasing recycled ink cartridges, and this fact can become your most convincing marketing tool for landing new business. Offer clients fast free pickup and delivery right to their offices, stores, or homes, and don't be afraid to go after the large accounts with lots of machines that need ink and toner cartridges renewed regularly. Additional information about starting your own cartridge recycling business can be sought by contacting the American Cartridge Recycling Association at ☎ (305) 539-0701.

Compile Mailing Lists

For many companies peddling highly specialized products and services, the only viable means of marketing is via print or electronic direct mail. Therefore, a great opportunity is available for computer- and internet-savvy young entrepreneurs to profit by compiling and renting their print and electronic direct mail lists. Mailing lists can be rented by creating self-adhesive mailing labels for direct mail print campaigns, or server-based electronic lists for electronic direct mail campaigns. There are a few ways that you can collect contact information about people and businesses to build your lists. One type is opt-in mailing lists, which are compiled from e-mail addresses of people who have given permission to be included. Another are subscription lists, which are composed of individuals and businesses that subscribe to print or electronic publications, such as magazines, newsletters, trade journals, industry reports, newspapers, and electronic magazines. A third are attendee mailing lists compiled of people that have attended a specific event, from seminars, trade shows, sports events, concerts, and workshops, to timeshare pitch sessions. Assembled mailing lists round out the top four methods; these lists are compiled from various published information sources such as telephone directories or industry association directories. The key to success in this business is quality. Well-targeted mailing lists rent for substantially more than junk lists, and the vast majority of mailing lists available definitely fall into the junk category. You will need to create a data card for all of your lists. A data card is used as a sales tool to inform and entice marketers to purchase your lists instead of your competitor's lists. On the data card is information about the cost per one thousand names, the size and minimum order of names, a profile description outlining details such as the source of the list, history of the list, average value of orders, and hotline information like the kinds of products or services that people on the list recently purchased, as well as list usage restriction information. Mailing lists can be sold to business and marketers online, using direct sales methods such as e-mail blasts and telemarketing, or sold to list brokers that will rent your lists on a revenue share basis. To help compile and manage your mailing lists, there are a number of companies selling mailing list management software, such as Email Manager Pro, ♂ www.email-manager-pro.com, Email Marketing Software, ♂ www.massmailsoft ware.com, and List soft, ♂ www.lsoft.com.

8

PET-RELATED BUSINESSES

North Americans love their pets. In fact, sales of pet-related products and services are expected to top $50 billion annually by the end of this decade! So if you love animals, why not turn your passion for pets into a profitable business venture and cash in on the huge demand for pet products and services? This chapter features lots great ways that you can make a ton of extra cash by starting a pet-related business. Just think, you could make and sell specialty dog biscuits, walk dogs, pet sit, or even start a pooper-scooper service. There are lots of choices, as you will soon discover.

Specialty Dog Biscuits

There is a lot of money waiting to be earned making and selling specialty dog biscuits, which is the perfect opportunity for teens and young adults who love dogs and like to tinker in the kitchen. Profit margins are very high in this business because people are willing to pay for the best dog treats money can buy. I know because I am one of these people who blow a bundle every month pampering my pooch with high quality doggie treats. Also, as people in general have become more health conscious of their own diets, they have begun to scrutinize their pet's diets as well. Many are turning to buying naturally-made biscuits for their dogs, even though these cost much more than commercially mass-produced dog biscuits.

Making dog biscuits is easy; all you need to get started are dog biscuit recipes, healthy ingredients, biscuit molds or molded cutouts, a catchy name, and basic packaging materials. You can sell the dog biscuits you make in bulk to independent and chain pet food retailers on a wholesale basis, directly to consumers through online pet products marketplaces, at pet fairs, and/or from your home selling to dog-loving family, friends, and neighbors. The best way to find all natural dog-biscuit recipes is by searching the internet. You'll need to know about what foods are safe for dogs; for instance, onion and chocolate can be damaging to dog's health and should not be used in your biscuit recipe.

Clothing for Dogs

You can make a bundle of loot designing, making, and selling duds for dogs. Sweaters and rain jackets are sure bets as top sellers, but dog lovers around the globe are also buying designer doggie hats, goggles, shirts, booties, and scarves for their beloved furry friends. The materials for getting started are minimal—basic design and sewing skills, equipment, patterns, and fabric. You'll also need a bit of gumption to get out and pitch your fabulous designer fashions to pet shop retailers, especially if your ambitions are to establish wholesale accounts with chain and independent pet shop retailers. If not, there are still many ways to sell direct to dog owners, including exhibiting at pet fairs, online via dog-related web sites, mail order supported by newspaper and online advertising, and by establishing a doggie clothing boutique at home. As a dog owner, I can tell you that word travels fast among dog owners, and when one finds a great product for her pet she is quick to spread the word to other dog owners.

Tropical Fish

You can make a small fortune selling fresh-water and salt-water tropical fish, as well as supplies and related accessories such as glass and acrylic fish tanks, tank stands, canopies, filters, fish foods, lights, aquatic plants, skimmers, ornaments, and cleaning supplies right from your home (with your parents permission of course). All of these items can be purchased at deeply discounted prices from manufacturers, wholesalers, and tropical fish farms, such as Uncle Ned's Fish Factory, ☎ (508) 533-5969, ♦ www.unclenedsfishfactory.com, or by contacting the Florida Tropical Fish Farms Association, ♦ www.ftffa.com. This organization will put you in touch with tropical fish farms. In addition to selling from home, you can also sell tropical fish and related supplies on the internet through tropical fish marketplaces, eBay, or your own web site. In time, repeat and referral business will help keep sales and profits healthy. On a cautionary note, be aware that there are laws and regulations to comply with in terms of importing and exporting tropical fish. Research into these laws will be required if you are planning to import or export tropical fish. The Tropical Fish Net located online at ♦ www.tropical-fish.net, provides lots of helpful information about tropical fish.

Engraved Pet Tags

To get started making and selling engraved tags for pets you will need to purchase blank tags or make your own by purchasing flat metal stock and using tools such as power sheers or a band saw to create interesting tags in the shapes of bones, hearts, specific breeds, and more. Net Signs, found online at ♦ www.netsigns.net, sells blank pet identification tags in bulk at wholesale prices. Whether you buy blank tags in bulk or make your own, the equipment needed to engrave metal tags is cheap and widely available, and not much workspace is needed. In fact, you can even operate on a portable basis engraving tags for customers while they wait. Ideal locations include setting up at pet fairs, pet retailers on weekends, renting kiosk space at malls, and displaying at flea markets. Of course, engraved tags for pets can also be sold online and shipped to customers once completed. This simple manufacturing business has the potential to be very profitable as material costs are minimal and tags are quick to engrave, yet can retail as for as much as $20 each for names, contact information, and messages engraved on custom-designed tags.

Simple Products for Pets

With Americans spending more than $30 billion every year just on products for their cherished pets, you don't have to be a rocket scientist to figure out that big bucks can be earned designing, manufacturing, and selling all sorts of pet products. What types of pet products can you make? A few include furniture for pets, doghouses, cat condos, pet carriers, aquariums, pet toys, and designer collars and leashes. In fact, you can turn your passion for pets into a profitable pastime by manufacturing and selling just about any kind of product for pets imaginable. For the most part, no special skills are needed because all of these products are very easy to make with a little practice working with only basic tools and equipment. The products you do make can be sold online through internet pet products malls and eBay, and in the bricks-and-mortar world by renting table space at pet fairs, craft shows, and public markets. If you are very ambitious, there is also a potential to sell your products wholesale to pet product boutiques, pet shop retailers, veterinarians, and groomers, or at least consign a few products to test the waters. Start researching products and the marketplace at web sites such as the American Pet Products Manufacturers Association, ♂ www.appma.org, and The Pet Professor, ♂ www.thepetprofessor.com.

Dog Walking

A dog walking service is perfectly suited for young people with a love for dogs; you can make great part-time cash walking dogs before and after school and on weekends. There are numerous styles of multilead dog walking collars and leashes available that will allow three or more dogs to be walked at the same time without becoming tangled, and most types cost less than $100 to purchase. Buying this equipment is important because it will reduce frustration and enable you to walk multiple dogs at the same time, which in turn will increase revenues and profits, not to mention that in most areas of the United States and Canada, dogs must be on lead while walking in public spaces. Design a promotional flier detailing your dog walking service and distribute it to businesses that are frequented by dog owners, such as grooming locations, kennels, pet food stores, community animal shelters, and community centers. Also talk to all of the dog owners in your neighborhood and give them a flier to introduce yourself and your service. Dog-walking rates are in the range of $6 to $12 per hour, per dog. Again, walking multiple dogs at a time gives you the best income and profit potential. Additional information about starting a dog-walking service can be obtained by visiting the National Association of Professional Dog Walkers web site located at ♂ www.napdw.com.

Pet Sitting

Lots of people have dogs, cats, birds, and other types of pets that are not suited to be boarded at kennels or left with friends or family when the need arises, such as pets with chronic health conditions or exotic pets for whom finding suitable boarding is difficult. Likewise, many people prefer to have their pets stay in the safety and familiar surroundings of home, as opposed to an unfamiliar boarding environment. When these pet owners are away from home there is only one available solution—hire a pet sitter to come to their homes to care for their beloved pets while they are away. Sometimes this means having to stay with pets overnight or for even longer periods of time, but for the most part, you can simply check in on the pets two to three times per day (before and after school, and again at night) to feed them, walk them, and provide companionship. Market your pet sitting services by talking to neighbors, and through pet-related businesses in your community such as veterinarians, pet food retailers, dog trainers, dog walkers, and pet grooming services. Remember that many people also hire pet sitters for short periods of time—a weekend away, a night out, or time off for family events. Therefore, you will need to develop a fee schedule for both long- and short-term pet sitting jobs. Sign-out a copy of 📖 *Start Your Own Pet-Sitting Business* by Cheryl Kimball (Entrepreneur Press, 2004) from your local library for additional information about starting a pet-sitting business.

Pooper-Scooper Service

It may not be super cool, but believe it or not you can actually make great part-time money after school and on weekends operating a doggie pooper-scooper service in your community. This is an easy business to start requiring little investment, no special skills, and minimal equipment to operate. You will need reliable transportation (even a bicycle will work), a cell phone, garbage buckets, shovels, gloves, and a good pair of rubber boots, but that's about it. Basically, if you can handle a shovel, plastic bags, and can put up with less than aromatic smells, then you are qualified to start and run a pooper-scooper service. Most pooper-scooper services charge a flat monthly rate of between $30 and $60, which includes a once-per-week visit to clean up the yard, typically taking no more than 10 minutes. And if you guessed that "cleaning up the yard" means removing dog waste, you're right. Get the word out about your pooper-scooper services by talking to friends, family, and neighbors, and by running low-cost classified advertisements in local newspapers, pinning promotional fliers to bulletin boards, and by informing dog-related businesses in the community, such as pet food retailers, groomers, dog-walkers, and veterinarians about your service. Pooper Scooper, located online at ♂ www.pooper-scooper.com, is a directory of dog waste removal services and also provides lots of helpful information about starting and operating your own pooper-scooper service.

Dog Washing

Calling all dog lovers, here is your chance to tap into the highly lucrative dog grooming industry simply by washing dogs. This is a service that can easily be operated on a mobile basis going to your customers homes, or having them come to you. There are an estimated 30,000,000 pet dogs in North America, and most owners think nothing of spending a bundle on a regular basis to keep their pampered pooches clean. In fact, you can charge in the range of $10 to $15 for washing small breed dogs, and as much as $25 for washing large breed dogs. Not much is needed in terms of equipment and supplies to get started—access to warm water, buckets, lots of towels, and a selection of dog-friendly shampoos. Advertise your dog washing service by posting promotional fliers where they are most likely to be seen and read by dog owners, such as at pet product retailers, veterinarians' offices, and doggie daycare centers. This is very much an enterprise that will thrive on repeat and referral business. Therefore, smile, do a good job, and charge a fair rate, and you will probably have more work than you can handle.

Dog Obedience Instructor

If you love dogs and have some experience training the family pet, then you should know that dog obedience training is a multi-million dollar industry and growing every year as more and more dog owners realize the benefits of obedience training. You can start the business small and travel to your client's homes for training classes for one-on-one training. Or if you are really ambitious you can strike deals with schools and community centers and host dog obedience classes on weekends and nights, enabling you to train numerous dogs at one location. Many obedience trainers are currently not certified by a recognized association. However, if you really enjoy the work and are serious about making dog obedience training your post education career, I strongly suggest that you enroll in a professional training program and obtain a recognized dog obedience trainer certificate. Current rates for in-home training sessions are in the range of $20 to $40 per hour and many trainers create dog training packages for their customers, which include a set amount of training classes and course materials in print and video formats. A good book on the topic is 📖 *Expert Obedience Training for Dogs* by Winifred G. Strickland (Howell Book House, 2003). You can also log onto the Canadian Association of Professional Pet Dog Trainers, ♂ www.cappdt.ca, or the National Association of Dog Obedience Instructors, ♂ www.nadoi.org web sites to find out about certification programs offered in your area.

Sell Pet Toys

The millions of dogs and cats in the United States and Canada play with millions of chew ropes, buddy balls, Frisbees, bells, catnip mice, and other dog and cat toys of all kinds. To cash in on the pet toys craze, you will first need a reliable wholesale suppler. I would suggest that you contact The American Pet Products Manufacturers Association, ♂ www.appma.org, to get a list of companies manufacturing toys for pets. Companies such as King Wholesale Pet Supplies, ♂ www.king wholesale.com, and Purrfect Paws Wholesale, ♂ www.purrfectpaws.com, are also a good starting point because both sell pet toys at wholesale prices. Selling pet toys for profit can be accomplished in many ways—online sales, flea markets, pet shows, and vending at community events. Another unique way to sell is simply to visit parks frequented by dogs and owners. On any given day, and especially on weekends, you are bound to run into 20, 30, or more pets every hour, and you can start selling and handing out information about your business and how people and their friends can buy. That is a very effective grassroots approach to marketing and sales that works!

Pet Memorials

The loss of a pet is a very emotional experience for the owners. Many choose to purchase memorials that can be paced in yards or gardens as permanent reminders of their cherished friends. Making and selling pet memorials is a fantastic business for young and ambitious people to start. Pet memorials are similar to people memorials—a stone marker inscribed with the pet's name, a message, and often an image of the pet. You can use natural field or river stone, granite, marble, or whichever type of stone your customers choose. Check the Yellow pages under "stone supply" or "landscape supply" to find a rock dealer in your area. You will need to purchase a sandblaster (and safety equipment) and teach yourself how to use it, but don't worry, the learning curve is short. If you have the creative abilities, you can design and cut the stencils used in the sandblasting process. If not, hire an art student (perhaps a friend) to draw and cut the stencils. The best way to market pet memorials is to make sample markers, which can be displayed at veterinarians' offices and pet shops along with price lists and order forms. Customers simply complete the form and include the information and image they want on the memorial, and you fill the order, and deliver the completed memorial to your dealer, or directly to the customer by courier.

9

OUTDOOR-RELATED BUSINESSES

This chapter will appeal to you if you love to be in the great outdoors because you will learn about the best ways to make a ton of money working outside. There is something for everyone, regardless of your age. You can start a driveway sealing business, do farm work, hand deliver fliers, rake leaves, or if you have a green thumb, grow and sell specialty trees and shrubs. Even though some of the opportunities are seasonal, you can combine more than one venture such as tilling gardens in the spring and fall, with shoveling snow in the winter so that you can earn big bucks year round.

Make Money Tilling Gardens

Tilling gardens—grinding up the soil—is a very simple seasonal enterprise that pays well. You will need to invest in a roto-tiller, as well as a truck or trailer for transportation. Or, concentrate on tilling gardens close to home, so that transportation is not an issue. Tilling the garden performs a number of necessary functions, such as mixing organic matter and fertilizer into garden soil, and it helps to control weeds that compete with vegetables for moisture and nutrients. Most gardening gurus agree that it's important not to over till a garden. Twice a year is good, once in the spring before planting and again in the fall after all vegetables have been harvested. Advertise the service by talking to friends, family, and neighbors, and by posting fliers at garden centers and community bulletin boards, and also by running low-cost classified ads in your local newspaper in the spring and fall. Join gardening clubs to network with potential customers. Do a good job and you will have customers calling you year after year. Expect to earn in the range of $15 to $25 per hour. If mom and dad don't already have a tiller that you can use, the best way to find a secondhand garden tiller in good working condition is to check classified ads in your local newspaper and go to garage sales and auction sales.

Board-Up Before a Storm

Hurricanes, tornadoes, tropical storms, blizzards, and gale winds can cause millions and sometimes even billions of dollars worth of property damage every time one of these weather phenomenon happens. No one can prevent them; you can, however, help home and business owners be more prepared when the weather does turn foul by starting a simple window board-up service. Board-up work is actually quite simple. All you need to do is to go to your client's home or business and measure all windows. The next step is to cut plywood panels to fit each window, label each panel for the corresponding window, install quick assembly hardware on the exterior window trim, and presto, the next time the weather turns ugly, your customer can board-up his windows in a matter of moments. The boards can be stored when not needed, and when the need arises each is already the right size, clearly marked, and ready to install, which means no long waits at the lumber yard with hundreds of other anxious people trying to buy plywood and fasteners to board up their windows before the storm hits. The best way to market this unique business is to simply get out and knock on doors telling people about the benefits of your service. It should not take long until referral business kicks in and makes up the lion's share of new business.

Seal Driveways

Sealing driveways is the perfect opportunity for young people looking to work flexible hours and earn an excellent income. Sealing or coating asphalt driveways is an easy four-step process:

1. Edge the driveway, removing grass, weeds, and loose debris.
2. Fill cracks with cold asphalt compound.
3. Power sweep, compressor blow, or power-wash the driveway surface clean.
4. Apply the premixed asphalt sealer.

There is self-propelled and tank-feed spraying equipment available at relatively reasonable costs, which makes the job less labor intensive. If you are on a tight start-up budget, you can use the good old Armstrong method and simply roll on the sealer straight from a five-gallon bucket using a coarse roller or squeegee. There are also contemporary acrylic driveway sealers available in a wide range of colors so you can even offer to match your client's driveway color to the color of her house siding, trim, or even car. This is important because you are not limited to sealing only older driveways in need of a spruce-up, but any driveway is a potential candidate if the homeowner would like to change its color. You will find necessary driveway sealing supplies and equipment at most major building centers, or you can shop online at web sites such as, Seal Master, ♂ www.sealmaster.net. On average you can earn between $25 and $40 per hour sealing driveways on weekends. Additional information about sealing driveways can be found online at Driveway Tips, ♂ www.drivewaytips.com.

Hand Deliver Advertising Fliers

A flier delivery service is very easy to start and operate and can generate a great part-time income, which makes this a great moneymaking opportunity for entrepreneurial kids and young adults. Only a telephone and a good pair of walking shoes are needed to start. Business owners have long utilized promotional fliers as a fast and frugal, yet highly effective, way of advertising their products and services. They are cheap to print and you can fit an enormous amount of promotional information, pictures, and contact details on one flier, especially if both sides are used. Flier delivery services typically charge in the range of 5 cents to 10 cents for each flier individually hand delivered. But to increase profits, simply deliver more than one flier to each home. By delivering five fliers for separate business clients, all in the same area, you could be raking in up to 50 cents per delivery and spending less than 30 seconds to get the job done (that's $60 an hour if you don't stop). And during busy times you can even make more money by hiring your friends to also deliver fliers and splitting the revenue with them. Creating your own flier describing your service as well as rate information, and delivering it to businesses in your community is the easiest way to get the telephone ringing and clients lining up to get their promotional fliers hand delivered by your fast, friendly, and reliable service.

Trees and Shrubs

You can earn big profits growing specialty trees and shrubs right in your own backyard, providing mom and dad don't mind. Best of all, you don't need a green thumb or a lot of cash to get started. Surprisingly, not much space is required to make extra cash growing trees and shrubs. In fact, a 20-foot square garden plot is large enough to support 300 seedlings, which in turn can produces approximately 100 saleable trees annually when planting is alternated. Wow, that is as much as $5,000 every year from just a small patch of ground in your backyard. Seedlings, such as Japanese maple will cost about 75 cents each wholesale, which can be planted in pots or burlap and resold after a season or two for as much as $25 to $50 each. Now just imagine what you can earn by planting a 50-, 60-, or 100-square foot seedling tree garden. Selling the trees and shrubs is easy: Simply erect a "Trees for Sale" sign in front of your home on weekends, or pot some up and rent vending space at garden shows and flea markets. You can also sell the trees and shrubs to garden centers and landscape contractors wholesale. There are a number of wholesale nurseries and tree farms that will ship seedlings directly to your home at deeply discounted prices. A few of these include Mike's Backyard Growing System ♂ www.freeplants.com/starting-a-plant-nursery.htm, May Trees, ♂ www.maytreeenterprises.com, Brooks Tree Farms ♂ www.brookstree farm.com, and Meadow Lake Nursery, ♂ www.meadow-lake.com.

Painting Lines

Line painting is needed in parking lots to distinguish stalls, handicap zones, directions, and reserved spaces. Line painting is also needed for sports fields and running tracks, temporary marking for special events, and interior uses for marking traffic zones and directions in warehouses and factories. In short, lots of painted lines and directions are needed. Walk-behind paint striping machines for both pavement and turf marking are available for a relatively modest cost, in the range of $1,500 to $5,000, along with reusable stencils for marking. There are a number of companies selling line painting equipment and supplies online, such as Fast Line ♂ www.fastline.net, Seal Master ♂ www.sealmaster.net, and Trusco Manufacturing

⚘ www.truscomfg.com. In addition to line painting equipment, you will also need a truck or trailer to move equipment from jobsite to jobsite, as well as a power washer or blower to clean surfaces before applying traffic paint. An initial invest of less than $10,000 will get you started. Potential customers include commercial property owners, property managers, developers, and warehouse owners, as well as sports field and running track contractors, paving contractors, sports clubs, and schools. This is a great opportunity for young entrepreneurs wanting to earn in excess of $25 per hour working weekends and during the summer holidays. Line painting is an easy skill to learn and the service is always in demand.

Handyperson

Cash in on the multibillion-dollar home repair industry by starting your own simple handyperson service. Don't worry if your handyperson skills are limited, because homeowners always have lots of little jobs to be done that require little skill. Everyone is qualified to do things such as painting a garage, fixing fence boards, or installing storm windows. Of course, if you do have advanced skills in carpentry, plumbing, and electrical, then you can offer a wider base of handyperson services and charge more. Currently, handyperson billing rates are in the range of $15 to $40 per hour, plus materials and a markup to cover the costs associated with handling and delivery. You will need access to reliable transportation, or work close to home, and you will also need to purchase basic tools or borrow them from dad's workshop, but that's about all you need to get started. The service can be promoted and marketed to both residential and commercial clients by running cheap classified advertisements and by delivering promotional fliers to homes in your neighborhood. Repeat business and word-of-mouth referrals will become your main source of new business once you are established, providing you offer clients good value and excellent service. To advance your skills and increase what you have to offer, check out your local home improvement stores like Home Depot and Lowe's for what they are offering for free do-it-yourself classes.

Human Billboard

If you are looking for a fun way to earn lots of part-time cash, then becoming a human billboard is definitely the right moneymaking opportunity for you. We have all seen them, people in wacky costumes holding sings or banners emblazoned with promotional messages in high-traffic areas of the community—usually outside, in front of, or in close proximity to the business they are promoting. These people are called human billboards and they advertise everything from retail store sales to car dealerships to restaurants to homes for sale. The objective of a human billboard is simple: grab the attention of passing motorists and pedestrians and get them to visit the business or the event being promoted. Getting started in this business is also simple. Start by setting appointments with local business owners to explain your service and why they should hire you to promote their next sale or event. You will need to invest a bit of money in different types of wacky costumes, or you can rent them at first and buy them once profits start rolling in. This is the type of business that thrives on referrals and repeat business. Therefore, once you are established and busy, you can hire your friends to also dress up in wacky costumes and help out during busy times. Rates for human billboards vary, based on factors such as the number of people (billboards), the length of the promotion, and other items like signage and special costumes.

Beach Rentals

Renting fun items at the beach is not just a great way to relax for the summer, but it can also be very profitable. The business can be established at any busy tourist beach area, either from a fixed location or a portable one right on the beach with permission and permits. If the perfect location is not available or is too costly, you might try to partner with an existing business such as a hotel or restaurant, utilizing some of their outdoor space for rental purposes. The hottest rental items include inflatable inner tubes, shade umbrellas, open kayaks, snorkeling equipment, and boogie and surfboards. Additional revenue can be earned by providing quick surfing and snorkeling lessons if you have the skills, or you can always hire a friend with the needed skills. Even though start-up costs can be high because you have to purchase the items before you can rent them, the profit potential is outstanding, as many of the rental items will return their initial purchase cost within as few as six rentals, which in some instance will be your first week in business.

Snow Shoveling

Depending on your investment budget and how much money you want to earn, there are basically two methods for removing snow from walkways and driveways and de-icing surfaces during winter months. One option is to purchase a self-propelled snow blower as well as a manual salt spreader for de-icing. Both pieces of equipment are walk-behind models and would require a truck or trailer to move from job to job if you plan on working far from home. This allows you to make more money because you can do the work quicker and service a larger customer base. The second option is the good old Armstrong method. Armed with nothing more than a $20 shovel and bag of salt, you can shovel snow and de-ice surfaces by spreading the salt by hand. If funds are tight, then this is the best way to get started. Regardless of the option you choose, snow shoveling and surface de-icing is an easy service to start, operate, and sell, mainly because shoveling snow is hard work and you'll find lots of property owners will to part with a few bucks so they do not have to do it themselves. Even though this is a seasonal and weather-dependent opportunity, it is not uncommon for motivated young people to earn as much as $100 per day and more when the snow blows. You can also earn more money and work year-round by offering customers additional services like garden tilling, grass cutting, and light yard maintenance.

Raking Leaves

Okay, so you might not get rich raking leaves, but you can earn as much as $100 a day raking and bagging leaves for a month or so each fall. This opportunity requires little in the way of explanation, other than to say that raking leaves is hard work that requires a strong back. On a positive note, start-up funding requirements are minimal—a rake and a pair of gloves and you're in business. Securing customers is as easy as taking a walk in the neighborhood and knocking on doors to offer your service. Generally, you will find property owners are very eager to part with a few bucks to have their leaves raked and bagged. I would suggest that you charge in the range of $10 per hour for the service, plus the cost of bags. You can also earn more money and work year-round by offering customers additional services like garden tilling, snow shoveling, grass cutting, and light yard maintenance.

Wall Murals

Many business owners are having wall murals painted on large areas of their buildings, both on interior and exterior walls. The reason is because wall murals make excellent promotional advertising for their businesses, and are definitely something that customers will remember. Sometimes they just want to add a decorative element to their businesses, especially restaurant and flower shop owners. If you have the ability, or can form a group of young people with the ability to produce attractive wall murals, then you can make a lot of money operating your own custom wall mural painting service. Paint your first wall mural for free (with permission of course) and use the finished product as your "business card" to land new work. I will guarantee that no one else has a presentation portfolio like it. Approach businesses with photographs of your work. Additionally, bring a few suggestions and rough drafts of the wall murals you are proposing for their locations to show during presentations. It may take a few stops and presentations, but soon your wall mural art services will be in high demand. You will also have to get comfortable in your estimating skills, as each new job is unique. However, on average try to base your rates on an hourly fee of perhaps $20 to $30 per hour, plus paint and supplies.

Cutting Grass

Did you know that you can earn as much as $100 a day simply by cutting grass? How? By cutting five lawns a day and charging an average of $20 each. And, if you have the skills and equipment, you can also offer clients additional services such as rubbish removal and tree and hedge trimming, as well as seasonal services like leaf raking, garden tilling, and snow shoveling and make even more money. Most of the equipment needed to cut grass and operate a yard maintenance service is relatively inexpensive to purchase, especially if you buy used equipment or rent what you need until you earn enough money to buy your own. In fact, cutting grass was my first business, which required nothing more than a $5 investment to buy a rusty old lawnmower. On average you should have no problem charging in the range of $20 to $30 per hour. Providing you offer great service, and because cutting grass and general yard maintenance is hard work, there should be no shortage of homeowners eager to part with a few dollars per month to have their grass and yards kept in tip-top condition.

Newspaper Delivery

It might not be glamorous, but delivering newspapers can be a great way for young people to generate a steady income for many years. Having a plain ordinary suburban route can generate plenty of pocket money, but if you are ambitious, try to land a larger route that includes businesses, hotels, and apartment buildings because you will be able to deliver way more papers in the same amount of time, which means that you will be able to make more money and tips, especially around Christmas. The only investment you need to make to start delivering newspapers is proper clothing, namely comfortable shoes, rain gear, and a heavy jacket for the winter. To get started, contact your local newspaper to inquire about available routes. If you are serious, take what is available, even if it is not your first choice, because in time other routes will become available, and if you are reliable and dependable then you will have no problem moving up into these better routes. Because route size varies, as well as paper delivery frequency, there is no one rate to give, but if you are delivering papers five to seven days a week, it is possible to earn up to $500 per month.

Mobile Paint Spraying Service

This moneymaking opportunity brings paint spraying services to your clients. You can use an enclosed trailer or truck to house paint and equipment, or as a mobile paint-spraying booth. Or you can paint items outside by creating a mini-paint-spraying booth with portable walls. Mobile paint spraying services can be marketed to homeowners and business owners. A few items that can be spray painted for profit include: fencing, siding, garden equipment, appliances, handrails, flag poles, metal roofing, iron and plastic patio furniture, steel and wood boats, signs, utility trailers, metal sheds, construction equipment, concrete floors and walls, and outdoor swing sets. Design a basic promotional flier describing your service and deliver it throughout the community. Also rely on cheap classified ads to get the telephone ringing. Total start-up costs will vary depending on transportation needs. Paint spraying equipment is relatively cheap to buy and you can always buy used, or rent equipment as needed until you can afford to buy it. The income potential will also vary depending on what you are painting, but expect to earn in the range of $20 per hour plus materials.

Freelance Farm Worker

Young people living in the country or close to the country can easily make extra money working at local farms during the summer, before and after school, and on weekends. There are lots of farmers who need help to stack hay bales, pick rocks, clean barns and animal pens, do light repairs and maintenance, and even groom animals. But don't fool yourself into thinking that this is easy work, because it is not. Farm work is often very labor intensive and will require you to be fit and have the ability to lift heavy objects. But on the flip side, the pay is often very good, in the range of $8 to $15 per hour depending on the task. Getting work is easy. Print a business card listing your name and contact information on the front, along with any experience or the jobs you will to do printed on the back of the card. Once this is done, simply go for a drive in the country. Visit farmers and explain that you are reliable and are prepared to work hard, and you will soon discover that you will probably have more work than you can handle.

Paint House Numbers on Curbs

Painting house numbers on curbs is a fantastic moneymaking venture that any young person can start. The business is really that simple: paint house numbers in reflective paint on the road curb in front of the house. The purpose of this is so that in the event of a 911 call, the emergency personnel can locate the house easier, day or night. Also, numbers on the houses themselves or on mailboxes and lampposts often become hidden by overgrown trees and shrubs; having the numbers clearly and professionally painted on the curb makes life much easier for home deliveries and visitors to spot. The only equipment required is a set of good quality vinyl number stencils, reflective paint, and a paintbrush. Market the service by designing a promotional flier that details the benefits of your service, and start delivering them to houses in your neighborhood. This is the type of business that can be summed up as a numbers game—the more fliers you deliver and the more doors you knock on, the more house numbers you will paint. Charge customers in the range of $5 to $10 each.

Kindling Sales

Young adults can earn excellent profits by splitting, packaging, and selling fireplace and campfire kindling. Best of all, this business requires nothing more than a sharp axe and a strong back to get started. You can simply purchase firewood by the cord to split into kindling. Or you can be a bit more creative and get lumber for free that can be split into kindling. How? By visiting construction sites, wood mills, and furniture manufacturers and offering to haul away their waste woods and cut offs for free. Likewise, a walk through any forest will reveal lots of dead ground wood for the taking (with permission from the landowner of course). Once you have split the wood into kindling, it can be shrinkwrapped in plastic for retail sales. Ideally, you will want to sell the packaged kindling in bulk at wholesale pricing. Perfect locations for setting up wholesale accounts include RV parks, campgrounds, gas stations, and grocery stores. If you work to get waste wood for free for your kindling, the profit potential is excellent, as the only hard costs to produce the product are packaging and transportation to get it to the stores.

Wind Chimes

If you are looking to start a simple, yet potentially profitable part-time enterprise, you'll be glad to hear that no special skills are needed to design, make, and sell wind chimes. Likewise, tool and equipment requirements to make wind chimes are minimal. Beautiful sounding and aesthetically pleasing wind chimes can be constructed from a wide range of materials including bamboo, anodized aluminum, copper, stone, cast iron, glass, seashells, and ceramic tiles. And you can design and build them in just about every size, style, and price point imaginable to suit every individual's tastes and budget. Sell your wind chimes through online marketplaces such as eBay or internet malls, by displaying your products at craft shows and weekend flea markets, and by renting kiosk space at malls and public markets, especially close to Christmas.

10

BUY AND RESELL PRODUCTS

Buying and reselling new and used products is a great way for young entrepreneurs to earn extra cash. All you have to do is buy new or previously owned products that we all need, use, or want, and resell them for more than what they cost you. The difference between what you paid and what you sold it for, of course, is your profit: *Buy low, sell high.*

One of the best aspects about starting this type of moneymaking enterprise is that everyone is qualified. Buying and reselling knows no boundaries; you can be successful regardless of age, experience, education, and financial resources. Additional advantages include low investment, minimal financial risk, incredible profit potential, and very flexible work hours.

The proliferation of the internet also gives young entrepreneurs access to a global audience of buying consumers. The internet has not only made it easier to sell products into the global marketplace utilizing online sales venues such as eBay, e-commerce web sites, e-classifieds, and e-storefronts, but also to find sources for a nearly limitless number of in-demand products, which can be bought from domestic and overseas suppliers cheaply and resold for a handsome profit.

Selling New and Used Books

Buying and selling new, used, and rare books presents a fantastic opportunity for kids, teens, and young adults to earn extra money. New books can be purchased from book distributors, wholesalers, liquidators, retailer returns, and direct from publishers at deeply discounted prices that often reach 80 percent off cover price. A few sources for buying new books include the Independent Publishers Group, ♂ www.ipgbook.com, Ingram Book Group, ♂ www.ingrambook.com, National Book Network, ♂ www.nbnbooks.com, and Baker & Taylor, ♂ www.btol.com. One of the best ways to sell new books is on Amazon at ♂ www.amazon.com, alongside the books they sell, but for slightly reduced price to entice people to buy your books. Additionally, new books can be sold through other online venues and in the bricks-and-mortar world by renting table space at flea markets and mall kiosks. In terms of used books, there are an infinite number available to be purchased at rock-bottom prices. You can buy at garage sales, flea markets, online marketplaces, auctions, estate sales, library sales, and secondhand shops. Even better, few people take the time to find out the true value of the books they are selling, and because of this, many rare and valuable first editions, antique, and author-autographed books can be purchased very cheaply. You will want to invest in rare book pricing guides, such as 📖 *Bookman's Price Index: A Guide to the Values of Rare and Other Out of Print Books* by Anne F. McGrath (Gale Group, 2004), and use these guides to make wise purchasing decisions. Whether the books you sell are run-of-the mill used books for $10 or rare ones worth hundreds, the internet is your best marketing tool. List books for sale on Amazon, ♂ www.amazon.com, Abe Books, ♂ www.abebooks.com, eBay, ♂ www.ebay.com, and Used Book Central, ♂ www.usedbookcentral.com, and at flea markets. You can find out more about rare book dealing through the International Rare Book Collectors Association located online at ♂ www.rarebooks.org.

Portable Electronic Devices

Just like the thousands of other people making big bucks selling portable electronic devices on eBay, other online marketplaces, mall kiosks, and at flea markets, so can you. CD players, DVD players, MP3 players, cellular telephones, electronic organizers, good old-fashioned boom boxes, and more are all red-hot sellers. The starting point is to find reliable sources for good-quality portable electronics that you can buy at rock bottom wholesale prices. Online wholesalers such as 1 AAA Wholesale Liquidators, ♂ www.1aaawholesaleliquidators.com, Dollar Days Wholesale, ♂ www.dollardays.com, and Open Box USA Wholesale, ♂ www.openboxusa.com, all sell portable electronics, but there are also many more as a simple Google or Yahoo search will reveal. Of course, the more you buy, the lower your unit price goes, which may enable you to undercut the competition and sell for less. Therefore, it may be wiser to specialize in one or two types of portable electronic devices to start. This is a very safe venture to start because almost all of the money you invest in the business is for actual inventory that you will resell, which means that there is very limited financial downside, but lots of upside profit potential. In fact, eBay reports that portable electronics are best-sellers.

Vintage Clothing Dealer

How can a young entrepreneur strike it rich in a vintage clothing business? Start by spending time on weekends scouring flea markets, garage sales, estate sales, and auction sales for vintage clothing and fashion accessories, such as hats, shoes, handbags, and scarves that can be bought at bargain basement prices and resold for big profits. Even vintage T-shirts with logos from the seventies can fetch as much as $100 each! But before you start buying vintage clothing to resell, you first have to know what to buy and how much to pay. You will need to educate yourself about vintage clothing and the value of vintage clothing and accessories. The best way to do this is to purchase vintage clothing pricing guides, such as 📖 *The Official Price Guide to Vintage Fashion and Fabric* by Pamela Smith (House of Collectables, 2001), and 📖 *The Vintage Fashion Directory: The National Sourcebook of Vintage Fashion Retailers* by Daniela Turdich (Streamline Press, 2002), which lists every vintage clothing retailer in the United States. Vintage clothing and accessories can be resold for a profit directly to collectors and vintage clothing retailers or through online vintage clothing marketplaces and eBay. Who knows, you might stumble across a pair of Levi blue jeans from the turn of the last century for a couple bucks at a garage sale and resell them to a serious collector for about $5,000!

Secondhand Sporting Goods

Calling all young sports enthusiasts that want to earn some extra cash, by buying secondhand sporting goods cheap and reselling them for a profit. Not only can you make some extra cash, but also this moneymaking opportunity is sure to be lots of fun. Just think about all of the used sports and fitness equipment that can be bought cheap and resold for a profit—golf clubs, hockey equipment, wind-surfers, kayaks, canoes, bicycles, hunting equipment, skateboards, trampolines, gymnastic mats, tennis rackets; and that's just the tip of the iceberg. Secondhand sports equipment can be purchased in many ways, including scouring garage sales, sports swap meets, estate sales, auctions, and through private seller classi-fied ads. And in most cases, equipment can be bought very cheaply because peo-ple that no longer have a need for it just want to get rid of it at any price so they can clear the clutter from their basements, garages, and attics. Used sporting equipment can also be resold utilizing many of the same methods you will use to buy it—online advertising, flea markets, sporting equipment swap meets, classi-fied ads, and even from home supported by repeat and referral business. There is also a big market for vintage and collectible sports equipment, and if you have an eye for spotting good buys, then this is definitely an area to investigate further.

Collectibles

Throughout America, Canada, and much of the world, stuffed away in dusty attics or forgotten in dark basements are literally millions of collectibles, worth many more millions to collectors around the globe. You can cash in on the col-lectibles craze by becoming a dealer buying collectibles low and reselling high. Be forewarned, collectibles is a very broad subject, and can include items such as antique furniture, antique toys, vintage advertising items, military collectibles, prints and posters, movie and theater memorabilia, vintage jewelry, watches, and clocks, as well as collectible kitchenware, nautical memorabilia, automobilia, and petroliana. With that huge range, you will need to specialize, so pick something that you really think you will enjoy. You will also need to invest in collectibles' pricing guides specific to the type(s) of collectibles you plan on buying and reselling for a profit. Finding collectibles at rock-bottom prices is not overly diffi-cult; it just requires that you invest time on weekends scouring garage sales, flea markets, estate sales, and auction sales in search of bargains. Selling collectibles is easy, because there is always a gigantic market for them. You can sell online via eBay and internet collectors' marketplaces, and on weekends and during summer months by renting booth space at flea markets and antique and collectors' shows. There are many helpful web sites about collectibles in general and specifically about getting started in your own collectibles buy-and-sell business. A few of these include the Antique and Collectibles Dealers Association, ⚅ www.antique-andcollectible.com/acda.shtml, Antiques Web, ⚅ www.antiqueweb.com, The National Association of Antique Malls, ⚅ www.antiqueandcollectible.com/naam.shtml, and The Online Collector, ⚅ www.theonlinecollector.com.

Weekend Garage Sale Business

Here is your chance to cash in on the garage sale craze. A garage sale business is very easy to start and make money from, regardless of your age. Get started by buying good quality used items at low prices. How, you might be wondering? By going to auction sales, flea markets, other garage sales, and estate sales on weekends to find products that you can buy cheap and resell at a profit at your own garage sales. This is a great business to start with mom or dad because it enables you both to share the work load, spend time together, and make lots of extra cash. The best items to sell at garage sales include power tools, hand tools, toys, sporting goods, kitchen items, glassware, things for babies, lawn and garden equipment, crafts and decorations, collectibles, books, music and movie discs, kids clothing, and adult designer clothes. Professional merchandising is also important. If you are going to regularly hold garage sales, invest in folding display tables, display cases on wheels for easy transportation, and even a portable gazebo tent to protect against both rain and sun on your customers and the merchandise. Once you have collected items to sell, hold your own sale every month. Believe me when I say that it won't take long for word to spread about your monthly sales because garage sale enthusiasts talk to other enthusiasts and word spreads quickly. There are numerous web sites with lots of information about garage sale buying and selling, such as Garage Sale Planet, ⚅ www.garagesaleplanet.com, and Garage Sales Daily, ⚅ www.garagesaledaily.com.

Flea Market Vendor

Becoming a flea market vendor provides a fantastic opportunity for young entrepreneurs to earn excellent profits on weekends and during the summer. It is not unusual for flea market vendors to earn as much as $50,000 a year working only a few days a week! Flea markets are big business. In fact, there are an estimated

750,000 flea market vendors peddling new and used products in the United States and Canada at more than 10,000 flea markets, bazaars, and swap meets, some of which attract crowds in excess of 25,000 a day. Some of the best new products to sell are dollar-store items, toys, hand and power tools, crafts, costume jewelry, sunglasses, auto parts, and novelty products, all of which can be purchased dirt cheap from wholesalers and liquidators. Some of the best secondhand products to sell are glassware, antiques, collectibles, toys, tools, children's clothing, vintage clothing, and books, but you will have to spend some time scouring garage sales, auctions, and estate sales to find good quality secondhand products to buy cheap that can be resold for a profit. Before you sign up to sell at any flea market or swap meet, do a little research by checking out other vendors to see what they are selling, how much they charge, how much are they selling, and how many are selling the same things as you? Also research customers—are they buying or browsing and how many are there? There are also many types of flea markets—weekends only, every day, summer only, outside under tent, open air, and inside in swanky building resembling mall retailing more than flea market vending. All have advantages and disadvantages. Booth rents vary widely from a low of $5 per day, to as much as $100 for single-day events. Other considerations include customer and vendor parking, electricity, phone lines for credit card and debit card terminals, on-site ATM machine, washrooms, food services, and overall organization. In most cases you will need a vendor permit and sales tax ID number; some flea markets also require vendors to have liability insurance. There are a number of online flea market directories, which are a good starting point for conducting research. A few of these directories include Flea Market Guide, ♂ www.fleamarket guide.com, Flea USA, ♂ www.fleamarkets.com, and Keys Flea Market, ♂ www.keys fleamarket.com.

Vending Cart Business

You can earn big bucks on weekends and during summer holidays by buying products such as T-shirts, crafts, art jewelry, sunglasses, watches, souvenirs, umbrellas, and hats at dirt-cheap wholesale prices and reselling them for a profit from portable vending carts. If you plan on selling from public lands and buildings you will need to contact your local city or municipal government to inquire about street vending opportunities. On federally owned lands or buildings, contact the U.S. General Services Administration at ☎ (877) 472-3779 or online at ♂ www.gsa.gov to inquire about opportunities. In addition to a vendor permit, you may also have to obtain liability insurance, a health permit, and fire permit depending on what you are selling. Vendors can work from portable kiosks and pushcarts or right from a suitcase depending on what they sell. You can rent, lease, or purchase new and used pushcarts and kiosks, which come in many styles and price points. Some can be towed behind vehicles or placed on a trailer for transportation, some are motorized, and others are pedal powered. Carriage Works sells new vending carts and they can be contacted at ☎ (541) 882-9661 or online at 🖙 www.carraigeworks.com. Likewise, the Cart Owners Association of America can also provide you with information about where new and used vending carts can be purchased or rented. They can be contacted at ☎ (559) 332-2229, or online at 🖙 www.cartowners.org. Remember, vendors can't be wallflowers. You must love what you do, what you sell, and be extremely comfortable talking with people.

Vintage Vinyl Records

Calling all young music enthusiasts that want to earn big bucks! You can buy vintage vinyl records cheap and resell them to collectors for big profits. Vinyl records have one of the largest followings of people who collect for hobby and listening enjoyment. Rock n' roll, jazz, country, blues, and big band, all are equally popular in 33⅓, 45, or 78 RPM format. They can sell for big bucks, especially rare first-run vinyl in mint condition. The best way to find vintage vinyl to buy cheap is by spending time on weekends searching through garage sales, flea markets, and estate sales. Typically, you'll find boxes full at every sale at prices of less than $1 each. Price guides such as 📖 *Goldmine Record Album Price Guide: The Ultimate Guide to Valuing Your Vinyl* by Tim Neely (Krause Publications, 2003), will assist you to determine value and condition. In addition to garage and flea market sales, you can also buy from online marketplaces and from private sellers who often use classifieds to advertise their entire collections for sale. Vintage vinyl can be sold to collectors through record collecting clubs, such as the Record Collectors Guild, 🖙 www.recordcollectorsguild.org, on eBay, at flea markets, and at music and collectible shows. Fortunately, there is no shortage of vintage vinyl to buy or people looking to buy. All that is required to succeed is finding the right vinyl at the right prices and reselling it to collectors will to pay top dollar. Vinyl Web, located online at 🖙 www.vinylweb.com, provides lots of helpful industry information and links to dealers and collectors.

Gift Baskets

There are two ways you can earn big bucks with your own gift basket business. First, you can purchase pre-made gift baskets wholesale and resell them for a profit. Second, you can purchase all of the supplies to create unique one-of-a-kind gift baskets from your own designs and sell these for a profit. Your decision will depend on your budget, the types of gift baskets you want to sell, and your target customers. If you decide to make your own, don't worry because gift baskets are easy to assemble and all of the products and the baskets are readily available from any number of wholesale sources, such as Bacon Basketware Wholesale, ♂ www .baconbasket.com, and Country Baskets Imports, ♂ www.basketsimports.com. Simply select items such as specialty foods, fashion accessories, cosmetics, candles and soaps, or flowers, arrange in attractive wicker baskets or similar containers, wrap in foil or colored plastic, and the gift basket is complete. I suggest that you concentrate your marketing efforts on gaining repeat corporate clients, professionals, small business owners, and sales professionals, such as real estate agents. Basically, focus marketing efforts on individuals and companies that would have reason to regularly send gift baskets to clients. You can also sell gift baskets at community events, from rented mall kiosks, flea markets, and public markets on weekends and holidays. 📖 *Start Your Own Gift Basket Service* by Jacquelyn Lynn (Entrepreneur Press, 2003) provides lots of helpful information about starting a gift basket business.

Fireworks

Besides being at least 18 years old, there are two major stumbling blocks to get past in terms of selling fireworks. First, can you legally sell fireworks in your state? Second, if you can legally sell fireworks, can you meet minimum storage and transportation regulations? From a federal perspective, you can legally sell fireworks classified as "consumer fireworks." Every state has further regulations about the sale, storage, and transportation of fireworks. Some, such as Arizona and Georgia do not allow the sale of any fireworks, while others like Iowa and Ohio allow novelty fireworks sales. Still other states such as Texas and Washington allow the sale of all consumer fireworks, including cone fountains, roman candles, sky rockets, firecrackers, sparklers, revolving wheels, and others. To find out more about the purchase, sale, transportation, and storage of fireworks, visit the National Council of Fireworks Safety at ♂ www.fireworksafety.com or call ☎ (301) 907-7998. Providing you can meet the legal requirements, buying and selling fireworks can be extremely profitable because you can purchase them at up to 50 percent off retail directly from manufacturers and lesser discounts from wholesalers. A few buying sources include Fireworks R Us, ♂ www.fireworksrus.com, HAMCO Fireworks, ♂ www.hamcofireworks.com, and Patriotic Fireworks, ♂ www.patfire.com. The best sales locations are temporary rental storefronts in highly visible and high traffic areas in your community, especially just before July Fourth, Labor Day, and Halloween. Once again, providing you meet the legal requirements, you can also sell fireworks at flea markets, from your own web site, and by mail order.

Gifts-in-a-Can

Making and selling gifts-in-a-can is a simple, unique, and potentially very profitable part-time moneymaking opportunity. Gifts-in-a-can are exactly that: a gift type item cleverly packaged in a quart- or gallon-size paint style can or similar packaging and sold to consumers or corporations. Great gift ideas include silk-screened T-shirts, stuffed animals, toys, pet products, dried flowers, and herbs. All of the parts necessary to make the product can be purchased cheaply on a wholesale basis—gifts, cans, and labels. You simple assemble the product by packing the gift in the can, sealing the lid, and applying the exterior label. The finished product can be sold wholesale to gift retailers, or directly to consumers via online marketplaces and by renting kiosk space at malls and gift shows on weekends. There is also a potential to supply corporations, business owners, and professionals with gifts-in-a-can, so they can give them away to their customers as appreciation gifts. In this instance you would simply pack the can with the gift of your client's choice and have exterior labels designed and printed to meet their marketing objective. Companies such as Dollar Days, ✄ www.dollardays.com, sells a wide variety of gift products at wholesale prices, and SKS Packaging, ✄ www.sks-bottle.com, sells wholesale paint tins. Both are good places to start your research.

Temporary Tattoos

Have fun and earn lots of extra cash selling temporary tattoos. Today's peel-and-stick tattoos rival the best authentic tattoos in terms of color and design, and can last for a week. Of course, there are two major advantages of temporary tattoos over their real counterparts: they are not permanent and they cost a mere fraction of the real McCoy. In fact, temporary tattoos can be purchased in bulk for as little as five cents a piece. Granted, at a retail price of $1 to $5 each you will have to sell a lot of them to make big bucks, but on the other hand, almost all of the money you do earn will be pure profit. A couple wholesale buying sources for temporary tattoos include, Dune Temporary Tattoos Wholesale, ✄ www .temptats.com, and Tattoo Manufacturing, ✄ www.tattoosales.com, although lots more can be found online. You will want to concentrate your marketing efforts on the main target market for temporary tattoos—kids and teens. Go to where kids congregate and set up a portable kiosk to work from. Excellent locations include the beach, and community events like fairs, flea markets, parades, and music concerts.

Part-Time Flower Kiosk

Hey young entrepreneurs! Did you know that providing you can secure the right high-traffic location, a fresh-cut flower vending business can be extremely profitable? In fact, markups of 300 percent or more are very common. Just think, buy a dozen flowers wholesale for $10, and you can resell them for as much as $30 retail! One of the best ways to sell fresh-cut flowers is from a portable or fixed kiosk. Many companies such as Carriage Works, ☎ (541) 882-9661 ♂ www.carriage works.com, design and sell professional flower kiosks, but if you or someone in your family is a handyperson, one can be constructed for less than a thousand dollars. Great operating locations include malls, transit stations, public markets, farmers' markets, and even in conjunction with larger retailers such as grocery stores or building supply retailers that do not currently sell fresh-cut flowers. Roses, mums, carnations, daisies, and other varieties of best-selling flowers can be purchased at rock-bottom wholesale prices from flower distributors such as Anthuriums International, ♂ www.flowersales.com, and Florabundance, ♂ www .florabundance.com. Depending on the location, fresh-cut flowers can be sold part-time on weekends or even just seasonally during Christmas, Valentine's Day, Mother's Day, and Thanksgiving.

Selling Christmas Trees

Many people want the look and smell that only a real Christmas tree can provide, regardless of messy needles, cost, and disposal issues. North American consumers spend more than $1 billion annually to make sure that they have a real tree decorated and ready for Christmas cheer. Of course, in order to sell Christmas trees you will need to buy them wholesale. Fortunately, there are many Christmas tree farms selling trees at rock-bottom wholesale prices, such as All Season Trees, ♂ www .allseasontrees.com, Alpine Farms, ♂ www.alpinefams.com, and Christmas Trees Worldwide, ♂ www.christmastreeww.com. Direct from tree farmers, bound Christmas trees cost in range of $10 to $40, depending on size and type of tree—fir, balsam, or jack pine. Retail prices also vary greatly, depending on the type and size of tree and the area where the trees are being sold, ranging from a low of $40 to more than $150. You can sell Christmas trees right from home, providing your parents and your neighbors don't mind. Another option is to rent an empty lot space from Thanksgiving weekend until Christmas Eve. Good locations include grocery store parking lots, busy intersections, gas station lots, and basically any other piece of empty ground that is exposed to lots of passing motorists. Even selling trees to family, friends, and neighbors can generate excellent seasonal profits.

Power Garden Equipment

If you have small engine repair skills and knowledge, then why not put them to profitable use by starting a power garden equipment resale venture. Purchase lawn and garden equipment such as lawn mowers, trimmers, riding mowers, chainsaws, garden tillers, yard trailers, snow blowers, and leaf blowers at garage sales, auction sales, and through classified ads, and resell them all for big profits. To get the lowest prices, buy equipment out of season or that needs minor repairs and a good clean up. Often it is possible to acquire these items for free if you are willing to pick them up, especially if they do not work. You can sell your products from home supported by local classified newspaper advertising, signage, and by posting fliers listing your equipment for sale on community notice boards. And remember that you will close more sales and for more money by offering customers a 30- or 60-day warranty on all equipment sold. Doing so will easily increase the value of each piece of equipment by 10 to 20 percent and put more profit in your pockets.

Comic Book Sales

Buying and reselling new comic books for profit is a snap. Simply start by buying top name publisher brands like DC, Marvel, Disney, and Gold Key from comic book distributors and publishers, and resell them online and through flea markets. Distributors include Cold Cut Comic Distributors, ✄ www.coldcut.com, and Diamond Comics Distributors, ✄ www.diamondcomics.com. The same, however, cannot be said for buying and selling used and vintage comic books. The industry is competitive, and you need a strong knowledge of comic books to succeed. The value of used comics is based mainly on rarity and condition. But they are only worth what someone is willing to pay for them, so it is critical to get them in front of the right people if you hope to sell for top dollar. *Comics Buyer's Guide* is the longest-running magazine about comic books, available by monthly subscription from Krause Publications, ☎ (800) 258-0929. Monthly issues feature new comic reviews, a monthly price guide, and comic convention news. 📖 *The Overstreet Guides to Comic Book Pricing and Condition* from Gemstone Publishing, ✄ www .gemstonepub.com, ☎ (888) 375-9800, is considered the industry standard in terms of rating comic book prices and conditions. Both are invaluable tools. You can sell through eBay and other online comic buy-and-sell marketplaces such as Comic Link, ♂ www.comiclink.com, and Vault Auctions, ♂ www.vaultauctions.com. The best way to find used and vintage comics cheaply is by going to garage sales and flea markets.

New Toys

Did you know that billions of dollars worth of toys are sold every year in the United States? And you can cash in big and earn excellent part-time profits buying new toys at wholesale prices and reselling them at full retail prices. There are a couple of ways to buy toys. The first is to buy from toy wholesalers and distributors, such as ESCO Imports, ♂ www.escoimport.com. The second way to obtain the absolute lowest prices is to buy direct from toy manufacturers, especially factory-direct from China. Of course, if you choose the second option you will need to buy more upfront, which means a larger initial investment. Visit the Toy Directory online at ♂ www.toydirec tory.com, which is a database listing toy manufacturers. Stick to dealing only in new toys because the value of used toys is too low, except for collector toys. The best selling options include online sales through eBay and internet malls, and by renting booth space wherever crowds gather, such as flea markets, consumer shows, community events, and mall kiosks close to Christmas time.

Coins and Paper Money Dealing

To make big bucks buying and selling coins and paper money you first need to educate yourself about their value and how they are graded by condition for valuation. That way when you find a 1937-D 3-legged buffalo error nickel for a buck at a garage sale, you'll know you have stumbled across a $150 find. The best way to get educated about coins and paper money is by studying price guides, such as 📖 *The Official Blackbook Price Guide to U.S. Coins, 42nd Edition* by Marc Hudgeons and Thomas Hudgeons (House of Collectibles, 2003), and 📖 *The Official Blackbook Price Guide to U.S. Paper Money* by Thomas Hudgeons (House of Collectibles, 2004). You should also subscribe to coin and paper money collectors' publications like *Coin World,* ♂ www.coinworld.com, which is an online magazine serving coin collectors and dealers. Timing often comes into play and deals can be had when there are no other interested parties to purchase. That is why it is important to spend time scouring garage sales, estate sales, auctions, private seller classified ads, and at flea markets for the best coin and paper money buys. When selling, use eBay and other online marketplaces such Heritage Coin, ☞ www.heritagecoin.com, as well as coin shows and by joining coin and paper money collecting clubs, so that you will have the ability to sell directly to collectors at premium prices.

Selling Stamps

Stamps have long been a highly-prized collectible for people from around the globe. In fact, it is the number-one collectible hobby in the United States. Millions of people are engaged in stamp collecting, which creates a fantastic opportunity for young people to capitalize on their stamp collecting knowledge, and profit from buying collectible stamps cheaply and reselling them for huge gains. Scan classified ads, garage sales, flea markets, online marketplaces, and stamp shows for stamps to purchase below value. Resell to collectors via auction sales, online marketplaces, stamp shows, and through specialty stamp publications. Stamp Show, located online at ☞ www.stampshows.com, provides a directory listing stamp shows worldwide. You will need to be well versed in stamp grading and values, but there are numerous price guides available to help you in this endeavor. The most popular stamp valuation guides are published by *Scott Catalogs*. They can be contacted at ☎ (800) 572-6885, or online at ☞ www.amosadvantage.com. Also make sure you join online and offline stamp collecting clubs so you will have the ability to sell your finds directly to other collectors. The American Philatelic Society, ☞ www.stamps.org, provides lots of information about stamp collecting, as well as useful links and resources.

Sports Memorabilia

Calling all young entrepreneurial sports fanatics! It is time to put your knowledge of sports to good use and make a bundle of extra cash by buying and selling sports memorabilia. If you know what you are doing, you can buy team jerseys, autographs, photographs, sports magazines, action figures, novelties, posters, ticket stubs, and sports equipment at bargain basement prices and resell to collectors and diehard sports fans just like you for big profits! You will need to devote time to rummaging through garage sales, flea markets, secondhand shops, online marketplaces, and auctions to find valuable sports memorabilia items that you can buy dirt cheap. But with that said, the time you spend can be time handsomely rewarded when you sell your valuable finds directly to collectors via online sports memorabilia web sites and auctions and directly from home supported by local advertising. Books such as, 📖 *Standard Catalog of Sports Memorabilia* by Bert Lehman (Krause Publications, 2003), provides lots of valuable information to help

grade and price sports memorabilia. Likewise, companies such as Leland's, ♂ www
.lelands.com, Steiner Sports Memorabilia, ♂ www.steinersports.com, and Superior Sports Auctions, ♂ www.superiorsports.com, provide opportunities to sell
sports memorabilia direct to collectors.

Trading Cards

The value of trading cards continues to rise year after year, and because of this,
it is never too late to jump in with both feet and grab your share of the lucrative
trading card market. In addition to traditional sports trading cards like baseball,
football, hockey, and basketball, there are a great number of people who also collect nonsports trading cards such as cartoons, comics, movie celebrities, science
fiction, space, automotive, wrestling, and military cards. Having an interest and
some knowledge in trading cards will help you get started. But those who do
not can educate themselves about the trading card industry by way of online
forums, trading card clubs and swap meets, as well as trading card valuation
guides. Price guides will be an important tool to help you evaluate both purchases and sales, so be sure to acquire up-to-date trading card price guides. New
prepackaged trading cards can be purchased from wholesalers and distributors,
such as Sportsline Distributors, ♂ www.sportslined.com, Diamond Comics Distributors, ♂ www.dia mondcomics.com, and Baseline Sports, ♂ www.bl
sports.com. Used cards can be bought from collectors, classified ads, auctions,
flea markets, garage sales, and numerous online trading card marketplaces, like
Sports Card Depot, ♂ www.card depot.com, which is an online trading card
buy-and-sell marketplace. You can also utilize many of the same venues for
reselling the cards for a profit.

Rocks and Gems

Calling all rock and gem hounds! It is time to start profiting from your knowledge
by buying and selling rocks, gems, and related supplies. Purchase rocks, gems,
equipment, and related supplies from wholesalers as well as directly from rock
and gem hounds like you who spend weekends scouring the countryside for
treasures hidden in the soil, river beds, and sides of mountains and sell to crafters,
costume jewelry makers, enthusiasts, and consumers looking for neat home and
office decoration items. Books like 📖 *Encyclopedia of Rocks, Minerals, and Gem-
stones* by Chris Pellant and Henry Russell (Thunder Bay Press, 2001), will help you
identify various types of rocks and semi-precious gems. And, there are also many
rock and gem wholesalers, such as Pike's Peak Rock Shop Wholesale, ♂ www.pikes

peakrock.com and Shor International Wholesale, ℰ www.ishor.com, where you can purchase at rock-bottom wholesale prices. Rocks, gems, and related products can be sold on eBay, at industry trade shows, and by renting vendor space at weekend flea markets. If there are no rock and gem shops in your city, consider opening one in your home with mom and dad's permission—a converted garage would make a fantastic rock and gem boutique.

Novelty Products

Novelty and gag products such as key chains, lasers, light-up pens, gag gifts, fake money, and pencil sharpeners in the shape of a train are some of the hottest and most profitable gift items to sell at flea markets. You can easily double or triple your money on every single sale. In addition to flea markets, you can also sell novelty items right from a rented kiosk at malls, at the public market, or during community events like fairs and parades. Novelty products and gag gifts are also well suited to sell through online marketplaces like eBay and internet malls and through print and electronic mail order catalogs. There are a great number of wholesale sources for novelty products, such as Crazy Discounts Wholesale, ℰ www.crazy discounts.com, Empire Discount Wholesale, ℰ www.empiredis count.net, and Lakeside Products Wholesale, ℰ www.lakesidenovelty.com. To locate more, conduct Wholesale Novelty Products keyword searches on any of the popular search engines or directories.

Flags

Flags are big business generating millions in sales, and you can easily cash in on the flag craze by starting your own part-time flag sales business. Because there are almost too many kinds of flags that you can sell—country, state, provincial, sports, marine, safety, historical reproduction, royal, military, organization, windsocks, auto racing, and handheld—you might want to specialize. Buy flags direct from manufacturers and wholesalers, such as American Flags Wholesale, ℰ www.american-flags-wholesale.com, Patriotic Flags, ℰ www.patriotic-flags.com, or Sav-On Wholesale, ℰ www.sav-on-wholesale.com. Or conduct a *Wholesale Flag* keyword search on any popular search engine or directory to find many more wholesale sources. There are almost as many ways to sell flags as there are different types of flags. You can sell directly from home, online marketplaces including eBay and your own "flag" web site, and by renting vending booth space in malls, flea markets, consumers shows, and community events such as the Fourth of July celebrations and Flag Day. Additional income can be earned by selling flagpoles, as well as flagpole installation services, which can be subcontracted to a local handyman.

Security Mirrors

In spite of the popularity of security video cameras, security mirrors will always be a popular choice because they enable shopkeepers to keep an eye on their valuable inventory, while still assisting other customers. Security and safety mirrors come in many styles and price points. Ranging from an inexpensive 18-inch convex mirrors, which retailers can purchase for about $75, to four-foot ceiling dome mirrors for large surface viewing that can cost upwards of $400, which is still substantially less costly than video surveillance cameras and arguably more of a deterrent to would-be shoplifters. Even though the retail prices are reasonable, you can easily generate 30 to 50 percent gross profit on each sale. Best of all: Any young adult equipped with a stepladder and cordless drill can easily install a security mirror in about twenty minutes. The best way to market the security mirrors is to design a simple brochure highlighting all the benefits and features, and call on businesses directly. Talk with shopkeepers and let them know that you are there to save them money. If they deter just one thief from shoplifting, there is a good chance they have already paid for one mirror, and if they deter ten shoplifters a month, the shopkeeper will be ahead thousands every year, which is a pretty persuasive sales pitch. Companies such as Brossard Mirror, ♂ www .brossardmirrors.com, Newport Glass, ♂ www.newportglass.com, and See All Mirror, ♂ www.seeall.com, sell security mirrors at wholesale prices.

11

FOOD-RELATED BUSINESSES

There are lots of ways to earn extra money by starting a food-related enterprise. You can operate an ice cream cart in the summer, start a catering service, or become a hotdog vendor, just to mention a few. What makes starting and operating a food-related business such a great choice for young entrepreneurs is the fact that since we all have to eat, food businesses are proven moneymakers and in many instances very quick and cheap to start. As is true with any new business venture there are hurdles such as business, vending, and health permits to overcome, but with a little research and effort all are easily acquired in every community.

Snack Vending

Snack vending is a multibillion-dollar industry in North America, and getting a piece of this very pie is easy: All you have to do is to find the right location(s) and install a snack vending machine. Look for locations in your community that are busy or that have a large number of employees, ideally more than 25 people. Good locations often include car dealerships, factories, office buildings, fitness clubs, and laundries, but be sure to ask upfront if the property owners expect a fee, which can range from 10 to 20 percent of your gross sales or a set amount each month, perhaps $50 to $100 for each machine. Once you have found the right location and reached an agreement with the landlord or business operator to install the vending equipment, you will be in the position to know which type of machine(s) to purchase and the kinds of snacks to stock—soda pop, chips, candy bars, gum, coffee, and even sandwiches. Typically, you can expect to mark up snack products by 300 percent for resale. New vending machines are expensive, so consider purchasing secondhand machines or renting machines to get started. This way you can expand the business and buy new vending machines from the profits you earn. There are numerous companies selling new and used vending machines and supplies. A few include 123 Vending Supplies, ♂ www.123vending.com, Universal Vending Supplies, ♂ www.universalvending.com, and Vending Connection, ♂ www.vendingconnection.com.

Growing Herbs

Here is a fun moneymaking opportunity that can be right for anyone because start-up costs are minimal and even a small backyard herb garden can generate lots of extra cash. Herbs can be divided into three primary categories: culinary herbs used in cooking, such as basil, sage, chives, dill, parsley, rosemary, and thyme; fragrant herbs used in potpourri and essential oils, such as, tansy, clove, rue, thyme, and chamomile; and medicinal herbs, such as borage, catnip, ginseng, pennyroyal, and valerian. Regardless of the types of herbs you grow and sell, they are always in big demand. The first step is to get educated about herbs and herb gardening, which can be accomplished by reading books on the topic, joining herb-growing clubs, and obtaining information about herb gardening online. Next, devise a plan outlining the types of herbs you will grow and how each will be marketed. The plan does not have to be sophisticated, it just has to outline the basics such as production costs, marketplace and potential, pricing, and selling methods. Herbs can be sold in a wide variety of ways, including direct to the customer as plants or as a finished product, wholesale sales to retail stores and bulk herb buyers, and selling direct to restaurants and catering companies. A very helpful book on the topic is 📖 *Start Your Own Herb and Herbal Products Business* by Rob and Terry Adams (Entrepreneur Press, 2003). Likewise, Herb Depot, located online at ♂ www.herbs-depot .com, provides lots of helpful information about growing and selling herbs.

Produce Stand

A roadside stand can be very profitable along a busy highway or in front of your (parents') home you can rent a booth at a farmers' market, or set upportable kiosk at a local flea market and sell fresh in-season fruits and vegetables during the summer and on weekends. The key to success in this business is location, location, and, location. Excellent locations for a vegetable stand include gas stations, industrial parks, busy intersections, and along roadways leading to popular attractions like the beach, garden centers, and public parks. Or again, even right in front of your own home providing your parents don't mind, you can meet zoning regulations, and visibility to passing traffic is excellent. The stand you work from needs to be nothing more than a basic framework covered by a tarp to keep the sun or rain off the produce. Of greater importance are signs to advertise your products and business, which should be large, colorful, and compel passing motorists to stop and buy. Be sure to place your signs well ahead of your stand to give motorists ample warning so they have time to stop. Buy vegetables directly from farmers, or farmer's co-operatives in your area, or from produce wholesalers, such as Eden Valley Growers, ♂ www.edenvalleygrowers.com, and Seminole Produce Distributing, ♂ www.freshveggie.com. Regardless of your buying sources, sell only the highest quality and freshest products available.

Spinning Cotton Candy

The process for making cotton candy has not changed for over 100 years. Cotton candy is made using a melted sugar and a cotton candy spinning machine. Liquid sugar is poured into the machine and as the machine spins the liquid is forced through tiny holes creating the spider web or floss thread effect. The candyfloss cools and is served on a cone or stick. Cotton candy machines are very cheap to buy—brand new tabletop models start at about $400, and full-featured portable cotton candy vending carts are in the range of $2,000. Used equipment is available for about half the cost of new. Companies such as Fun Food Depot, ♂ www.funfood-depot.com, Gold Medal

Products, ♂ www.gmpopcorn.com, and Old Tyme Food, ♂ www.oldtyme food.com, sell new and used cotton candy machines and supplies. Because the only ingredient in cotton candy is pure sugar, about 90 percent of every sale is pure profit! Working from a booth or portable vending cart, cotton candy can be made and sold weekends and during the summer at community events such as fairs and parades, as well as at flea markets, beach locations, sporting events, and just about any other place where children (and adults) gather.

Hot Dog Vendor

Hey young entrepreneurs, big bucks can be earned on weekends, holidays, and during the summer by selling hot dogs at community and sporting events, concerts, auction sales, at the beach, flea markets, and by setting up in parking lots of busy retailers such as building supply centers. What do you need to know in order to start making part-time cash selling hot dogs? The list is actually very short. You will need a hot dog cart, a vendor permit, a health board certificate, and food stock such as hot dogs, condiments, buns, and soft drinks. In total expect to invest well under $5,000 if you purchase a used hot dog cart, and in the range of $10,000 if you decide to buy a new hot dog vending cart. Although the start-up financing needs are higher than some moneymaking opportunities listed in this book, the return on investment is quick because it is not uncommon for hot dog vendors to make sales of $1,000 per day or more in busy locations and keep half after expenses. Just think, find the right location and you could easily pocket an extra $20,000 after expenses selling hot dogs this summer. There are a number of companies in the business of selling new and used hot dog vending carts and equipment, including All American Hot Dog, ♂ www.allamericanhotdog.com, American Hot Dog Carts, ♂ www.americanhotdogcarts.com, and Willy Dog, ♂ www.willydogs.com.

Popcorn

Like hot dogs, excellent part-time profits can also be earned by making and selling popcorn, which should be music to young entrepreneurs' ears. The best places to sell popcorn include community events, sporting events, concerts, auction sales, at the beach, and at flea markets. The list of supplies and equipment needed to start is also short: popcorn vending cart, vendor permit, a health board certificate, popcorn, and packaging. An investment of less than $5,000 will get you on your way to earning fabulous weekend profits. Classic Carts, ♂ www.classic-carts .com, and Pop Corn Guys, ♂ www.popcornguys.com sell popcorn vending carts and equipment and both sites are an excellent place to start your research. If you are really ambitious, you could establish a wholesale popcorn business by supplying retailers with prepopped and packaged popcorn. To get this arm of the business started, call on video stores, convenience stores, groceries, and gas stations to setup accounts: You supply the packaged popcorn and they sell it. If you choose this route you will need to invest extra money into addition popping and packaging equipment and supplies to get going, but you will also have the potential to double your sales and profits if you sell both retail and wholesale.

Snow Cones

Let's face it, nothing beats the summertime heat like a nice refreshing snow cone treat, which makes snow cones one of the better products for young entrepreneurs to make and sell for big profits. Snow cone equipment and vending carts are cheap. A top-of-the-line model with all of the bells and whistles will only set you back about $2,000. There are lots of companies selling snow cone making equipment and supplies, such as the 1-800-Shaved Ice Company, ♂ www.1-800-shaved-ice.com, Columbia Jobbing, ♂ www.columbiajobbing.com, and Gala Source, ♂ www.gala source.com. Just think, once you have your equipment and you are ready to go, you can offer customers more than 50 tasty flavors to choose from, plus you can make additional profits selling other treats such as soft drinks, candy bars, and potato chips. For the most part, this is a summertime business, which is perfect for students who want to work for themselves instead of working a minimum wage job during the summer break. Location, location, and location is the name of the game for any retail business and selling snow cones is no different. The best locations to set up are high-traffic and highly visible areas in the community, but some will require permission for the property owner, and often you will have to pay rent. The best locations include supermarkets, malls, sporting events, at the beach, concerts, fairs, parades, rodeos, and parks. There is also the possibility to contract to sell snow cones at corporate events, grand openings, retail sales events, and large family gatherings.

Catering

Young entrepreneurs with a love for food and incredible cooking skills can turn this opportunity in to a profitable goldmine by starting and operating a part-time specialty catering business. Weddings, Christmas parties, corporate meetings, anniversaries, graduations, grand openings, product launches, tours and trips, and just about any other type of social function or business event can be catered for big profits. Start small and cater events for friends and family while you hone your cooking, business, and marketing skills. You will need to invest in basic cooking equipment, dishes, and utensils, and have access to reliable transportation. When you do land a few big catering gigs, don't worry about people power, because cooking, serving, and bar staff can be hired on an as-needed basis, and additional revenues can also be earned by providing valet parking services, coat check services, and by renting party items such as tents, tables, chairs, and PA systems to create a more all-inclusive service. A good book on the topic of catering is 📖 *Successful Catering: Managing the Catering Operation for Maximum Profit* by Soni Bode (Atlantic Publishing Group, 2002), which provides an in-depth look at what is required to set up and operate a catering business.

Grocery Shopping Service

With an aging population, starting and operating a simple community grocery shopping and delivery service is a very timely opportunity that is guaranteed to keep you busy and earning excellent profits nights, weekends, and during your spare time. Customers can fax, call-in, or e-mail grocery orders to the supermarket or to you, and the rest is pretty easy: Pick up the groceries at the supermarket and deliver the order to your customers. You will need reliable transportation such as a hatchback car, as well as a small cash float to pay for orders. Once the groceries have been delivered you are reimbursed for costs plus your pickup and delivery fee. Seniors are not the only potential customers, anyone that is either too busy or who does not have transportation is also a potential customers. Advertise using classified ads and by delivering fliers to homes and by posting fliers on community notice boards. Once word is out about your convenient, quick, and affordable grocery shopping service you will probably have more work than you can handle. In addition to groceries, you can also provide shopping and delivery services for prescription medications, pet foods, takeout food orders, and trips to the hardware store.

Cake Decorating

Turn your love for baking up a storm in the kitchen into a profitable pasttime by making, decorating, and selling one-of-a-kind specialty cakes for occasions such as birthdays, weddings, anniversaries, retirement parties, and corporate events. Contact wedding planners, photographers, bridal shops, event coordinators, restaurants, and catering companies to let them know about the specialty cakes you bake and sell. Send them an occasional free cake bribe now and then, just to make sure they send business your way and not to competitors. You can also bake and decorate cakes in advance and rent kiosk space on weekends at farmers' markets, public markets, and community events to sell cakes. Baking and decorating specialty cakes can be very profitable because ingredient costs only makeup about 15 to 20 percent of the total retail-selling price. There are many companies selling cake making equipment and supplies online, such as A.J. Winbeckler, ♂ www.winbeckler.com, and Baking Tools Online, ♂ www.bakingtools.com. The International Cake Exploration Society is also a good place to start your research and they can be found online at ♂ www.ices.org. And, if you have limited cake baking experience books like 📖 *The Wedding Cake Book* by Dede Wilson (John Wiley & Sons, 1997) will provide many valuable tips and help you get started.

Handmade Candy

Everybody loves candy, which is why making and selling candy is a fantastic business opportunity. First decide what types of candies you want to make and sell—fudge, chocolate, taffy, hard candies, soft candies, or any combination. Making candy is easy, and there are many books available such as 📖 *The Ultimate Candy Book: More Than 700 Quick and Easy, Soft and Chewy, Hard and Crunchy Sweat Treats* by Bruce Weinstein (Morrow Cookbooks, 2000), to help you get started. You need candy making recipes, molds, ingredients, and packaging supplies. There are a number of companies selling candy making equipment and supplies, such as Get Suckered, ♂ www.getsuckered.com, and TCB Supply, ♂ www.tcbsupply.com. You can also contact the National Confectioners Association online at ♂ www.candyusa.org, to locate additional candy making equipment and supply wholesalers. You will also need to develop a strategy for selling the candy you make. One option is wholesale sales to convenience stores, grocery stores, gift retailers, and candy boutiques. There are also other ways to sell candies directly to consumers such as renting mall kiosks, selling from a vending cart at flea markets, community events, and farmers' markets, or selling candy online.

Honor Snack Box Business

Look no further than starting an honor snack box business if your goal is to operate your own business that has the potential to generate an excellent part-time income, not to mention the fact that you can get started with an initial investment of less than $1,000. Honor vending boxes are simply predesigned and colorful cardboard boxes that contain snack food items like candy bars, chips, and gum for sale on the honor system. This means there is a coin box built into the vending box that does not lock, and customers are expected to pay for their purchases on the honor system. Ideal locations to place these boxes are in small- to medium-sized companies with 50 employees or less. The vending boxes can be put in lunchrooms or reception areas, and are replenished with new snack items on a weekly basis. An honor system box vending business is a very wise choice for young entrepreneurs seeking to get into the vending industry on a limited investment basis. It is very inexpensive to construct or purchase the boxes for honor vending as opposed to purchasing and maintaining traditional mechanical vending machines. There are also way more locations that honor vending boxes can be located than traditional vending machines.

Selling Nuts

Just about any young person with a bit of gumption can start making extra money by purchasing peanuts and other assorted nuts in bulk, at wholesale prices, and repackaging the nuts into smaller quantities and then selling the packaged nuts to retailers on a wholesale basis. Or alternately, the nuts can be placed into retail stores and sold on a consignment or a profit share basis. The best types of outlets for nut sales include gas stations, pubs, convenience stores, and laundromats. You will need to invest a bit of money into your initial nut inventory, as well as packaging and marketing materials, in total, perhaps a couple thousand dollars. But the return on investment is quick as you can easily mark up your product for resale by as much as 200 percent. Nuts can also be sold directly to consumers at sporting and community events, like fairs, baseball games, auction sales, public markets, and even flea markets, providing yet another way to make extra money.

Fruit and Veggie Picker

If you live in close proximity to fruit and vegetable growers you can be assured of making lots of extra money working as a freelance fruit and veggie picker in season. Grapes, apples, oranges, pumpkins, strawberries—the list goes on and on. There are always lots of fruits and veggies that must be picked and sorted by hand. Granted the work is often labor intensive, but at the same time if you are quick, great money can be earned because most orchards and farms pay pickers on the total quantity they pick and not an hourly rate. This is a better system because you have the opportunity to earn a higher income than you normally would if you were paid by the hour, providing you work efficiently. Getting picking work is easy. All you have to do is visit farms and orchards in your area and inquire about picking opportunities. Again, because the work is labor intensive, many farmers and growers have a difficult time finding enough pickers.

Ice Cream Cart or Stand

An ice cream stand or even just operating an ice cream cart can generate enormous summertime profits for highly motivated young entrepreneurs who aren't afraid to roll up their sleeves and get to work. In fact, it is not uncommon for an established ice cream stand to generate profits in excess of $50,000 in a three or four month season, and ice cream cart operators routinely earn $50 to $75 per day, providing the weather is warm and sunny. If funds are limited, then operating an ice cream cart will be a better choice, mainly because there is no cost to get involved. You simply contact an operator in your area, such as Dickey Dee, and they provide the cart and ice cream inventory and you are paid a portion of your total daily sales. If you choose to open an ice cream stand, expect to invest upwards of $20,000. In terms of a stand, location is the key to success. Good operating locations for an ice cream stand include mall food courts, beach areas, or a small storefront on a main street. Additionally, an ice cream stand can also be operated on a mobile basis by converting an enclosed trailer or delivery van into an ice cream stand. A mobile ice cream stand has many benefits as opposed to a fixed location due to the fact that you can transport your business to areas where demand is greatest for the product.

12

TEACHING AND COACHING BUSINESSES

Turn your knowledge and expertise of a particular subject or activity into a moneymaking venture by teaching others what you already know. If you know how to dance, then offer dance lessons; if you know martial arts, then train others in self-defense techniques; or if you are a whiz in math, then tutor others for big bucks. The demand for learning is unlimited!

Personal Sports Coach

Turn your passion for sports into a profitable business. If you excel in ice hockey, football, baseball, basketball, boxing, golf, tennis, soccer, swimming, figure skating, track, skiing, snowboarding, cycling, curling, gymnastics, martial arts, or competitive diving, you can turn these experiences and skills into a profitable part-time business by offering one-on-one personal sports coaching services. Amateur sports coaching is a growing industry in all areas of North America. Amateur athletes from five to sixty-five are turning to individual personalized coaching to gain an advantage on the field, course, ring, hill, or pool. Parents are parting with up to $50 per hour to make sure their kids receive the sports coaching they need so they are not left behind. Adult athletes are also lining up to enlist the services of freelance personal sports coaches to help them improve their games, get more enjoyment from their sports, and decrease the risks of injury. And guess what? It doesn't matter if you're only a teen or young adult, because if you excel at a specific sport, others will gladly pay you to help them do the same. Market your sports coaching services by networking with parents whose kids are involved in athletics as well as adult athletes in the sports where you excel. You can also team with community centers, sports clubs, and fitness centers and offer classes through these facilities.

Music Teacher

If you know how to sing, play guitar, piano, drums, a wind instrument, or a string instrument well enough to teach others, then what are you waiting for? Trade on your musical talents and earn a great part-time income working nights and on weekends by teaching other people how to play your instrument of choice. Classes can be conducted one-on-one or in a group format at your home, at the student's home, or in conjunction with community programs, continuing education courses, or even an established music store. Expanding the business is easy because it requires nothing more than hiring other experienced musicians (perhaps your friends) to teach more students, and more students mean you will earn more money. In that situation you would split the profits with your other instructors. Music lesson rates vary depending on class size, skill level, and instrument, but on average, group lessons cost students in the range of $10 to $20 per hour, and one-on-one lessons in the range of $40 per hour plus the costs of instrument rentals or purchases, course materials, and sheet music. Alternately, if you prefer to teach music without the added work of operating a business, then freelance your musical teaching talents out to an existing music school and earn in the range of $15 to $25 per hour teaching students. The Music Teachers National Association located online at ♪ www.mtna.org provides lots of helpful information and resources for music teachers.

Dance Teacher

There is big money to be earned by teaching other people aged 3 to 93 your smooth moves on the dance floor. All styles of dance are popular—tap, highland, ballroom, ballet, swing, break, modern, disco, flamenco, or line dancing. If space is available, the most convenient way to get started is to open a dance studio right in your home (providing mom and dad don't mind). If not, you can operate your dance classes in conjunction with a suitable partner or partners who do have the space, such as a fitness center, community center, music shop, banquet hall, tavern, school, church, hotel, or a community college. Or even teach dance moves to students right at their own homes. There are lots of options. Expanding your dance business is as easy as hiring other dance instructors in the same style or new styles to teach students and work on profit-split basis. One-on-one dance instruction rates start at about $30 per hour, while group rates are less per student, but you can earn more by teaching more people at the same time. Market your dance classes by delivering fliers in your neighborhood, running cheap classified advertisements, and by listing with online dance instructor directories, such as Dance Net, ♂ www.dance.net, and Voice of Dance, ♂ www.voiceofdance.com.

Academic Tutoring

Mathematics, biology, English literature, science, and history tutors are in high-demand by parents to ensure that their children are receiving the best academic educations. Extracurricular one-on-one tutoring for their children is the way that most obtain this peace of mind. Capitalizing on your academic skills in your field of expertise means that you can start your own tutoring service and have an opportunity to earn between $15 and $30 per hour. Tutoring classes can be held at your home or at your student's home. In addition to general academic tutoring, English as a second language (ESL) tutoring has exploded in popularity in the past decade, both for new immigrants and foreign students who need to master English for job and study reasons. Once you've worked with a few clients, word-of-mouth will spread, and you may be able to expand your business greatly by employing a number of private tutors to help fill the demand. Helpful information about tutoring can be found online at the National Tutoring Association, ♂ www.nta tutor.com, as well as Tutor Nation, ♂ www.tutornation.com, which is an online portal bringing together tutors and students.

Self-Defense Teacher

Self-defense training is big business and anyone that wants and needs to feel safe and secure is a potential customer. If you think that you are too young to offer self-defense training services, think again. One of my karate instructors is only 16-years old, charges $25 per hour for private lessons, and has a waiting list a mile long! Of course, the more qualified and better your credentials are, the more your training services will be in demand. Depending on your self-defense specialty, classes can be conducted in group format, or a one-on-one basis at your school location or the client's location, including his home, business, or office. Never before has self-defense training been as popular as it is right now. Literally hundreds of thousands of people signup for new classes every month and are prepared to shell out big bucks to learn the skills they need to know to keep themselves and family members safe. Rates vary from a few dollars per hour, per student when training a group, to as much as $50 per hour when training one-on-one. Word-of-mouth advertising and referral business will be your best marketing tools. Therefore, let everyone know about your training classes and provide the best service possible.

Mobile Computer Trainer

Capitalize on your computer skills by starting your own mobile computer training service. The vast majority of computer training schools require students to come to their locations for training classes, but not every person or business that purchases a new computer, software, or other hardware device has time to attend classes to learn how to use the equipment. Herein lies the opportunity. Start a mobile computer training service, and train students one-on-one, or in group format on their own equipment at their homes, businesses, or offices. You can offer classes whenever you're not in class yourself, including nights, weekends, during holidays, and all summer long. The proliferation of technological advances and constant new streams of software applications and hardware devices means that there will always be lots of people in need of training or skills upgrading, so they can get the most benefit from their computer equipment and programs. Because students use their own computer equipment and software, the business can be started cheaply—basically for the cost of a notebook computer, software applications, marketing materials, and reliable transportation. Advertise your computer and software training services using promotional fliers and coupons, newspaper classified ads, and by networking around the clock. It also helps to build alliances with computer and software retailers who can refer your training services to their customers.

Day Camp Host

Here is an opportunity that will appeal to young adults that are planning a career in teaching. Mathematics, computers, athletics, acting, or arts and crafts, just about any subject or activity can be the basis for a day camp for kids' business. Camps can be held in a daylong format on weekends during school months and throughout the week in the summer. The main focus of this type of specialized kids' day camp business is to provide parents with an alternate choice for additional education and activities as opposed to traditional tutoring. The day camp can be run as an independent business or in conjunction with a community program or community center. Start-up costs for this kind of business will vary depending on the operating format, but expect to have to invest a couple thousand dollars to get things started. Likewise, also make sure to seek legal advice in terms of any regulations and certifications that may be required to operate a day camp for kids' business in your community prior to establishing the business. Profit potential is excellent, as you can charge in the range of $20 to $40 per day per student.

Cooking Teacher

Put your extraordinary cooking skills to work: fantastic profits can be earned by teaching others how to make unforgettably tasty meals, deserts, and appetizers. Operating from home or on a mobile basis, going to your students homes, you can teach students how to prepare fantastic meals. One-on-one, students pay $20 to $30 per hour to learn how to prepare gourmet meals, and about half that amount when three or more are taught at the same time. Needless to say, it does not take many students to earn an extra $1,000 per month working just a few nights and weekends. Start-up costs are also minimal because chances are you will already have everything you need (or mom and dad do) in terms of cookware and other tools of the cooking trade. Post fliers in grocery stores, retail shops, and at your local butcher shop advertising your classes. Once up and running, this is the kind of specialized service about which word spreads quickly so don't be surprised if you are inundated with more students than you can handle in no time. Books such as *The Gourmet Cookbook: 1000 Recipes* by Ruth Reichl (Houghton Mifflin Co., 2004), are great investments because they allow you to expand your teachable menus.

13

TRANSPORTATION BUSINESSES

I f you have a reliable automobile or have regular access to a reliable automobile, there are many ways that you can use your car to make extra money, and this chapter features some of the best ways to make extra cash using your car. Likewise, there are also great moneymaking opportunities for young entrepreneurs listed in this chapter that do not require a car, such as cleaning boats, washing cars, operating a pedicab service, and many more.

Boat Cleaning

If you love boats and are looking for a way to earn extra money on weekends and during the summer, then cleaning boats might just be the perfect opportunity for you. Boat cleaning is a very easy service to start because there are no special skills or equipment required to operate the business. Even better, the income potential is excellent because you can charge in the range of $20 to $30 per hour, which is not bad when you consider this business can be started for less than $1,000. Boat cleaning is also a very easy service to market and creating printed fliers describing the services you provide and a little bit of leg work to distribute the fliers at marinas and boating clubs is all that is required to get things rolling. If you have the equipment and necessary skills, you can also offer clients additional services, such as in-the-water bottom cleaning, sailboat rigging, haul-out bottom painting, and woodwork or brightwork refinishing. These additional services can command as much as $60 per hour! A good book on the topic of boat cleaning and maintenance is 📖 *Boat Maintenance: The Essential Guide to Cleaning, Painting, and Cosmetics* by William Burr (International Marine, 2000).

Car Washing

Here is a simple business enterprise that is perfectly suited for young people of any age with the added benefits of flexible working hours, low overheads, minimal start-up costs, and zero prior experience. Washing cars, trucks, vans, and other equipment can be done in the neighborhood or operated on a mobile basis, which means that you travel to your client's location—home, business, or office—and wash her vehicle. You need only basic equipment to get this business rolling, including scrub brushers, shop vacuum, rags, garden hose, and buckets. Promote with fliers, discount coupons, advertisements in your local newspaper, and through personal contact (knocking on doors). Talk with car dealers, construction companies, courier services, and other businesses that have a fleet of vehicles and equipment that need to be cleaned on a regular basis, and pitch the benefits of your service—mobile, quality, fast, convenient, and great value. Securing customers that can become repeat customers is the best way to go because it is ten times easier and more profitable to have repeat customers that will use your service regularly than it is to continually find new customers.

Pedicab Taxi/Tour Service

Pedal your way to big profits by starting a pedicab taxi/tour service. A ride through the park, a sightseeing tour, or a relaxing ride to a restaurant—tourists and locals love to take in the sights and sounds in a pedicab ride around town. Pedicabs are available in a wide range of styles, purposes, and price points. There are basic two-occupant models all the way to models that will accommodate six people, and even others for urban parcel delivery that are equipped with storage space and no seating. Pedicabs start at about $3,500 to buy new, and half that amount to purchase used. There are many manufacturers building and selling commercial pedicabs, such as Main Street Pedicab, ☞ www.mainstreetpedicabs.com, and Premier Pedicab, ☞ www.tipke.com. Ride rates are currently about $1 per minute, with a minimum charge of $5. The business can easily be expanded from a one-person operation by purchasing multiple pedicabs and hiring subcontract drivers (or your friends) to operate the bikes on a revenue-split basis. Also, don't forget to sell the highly visible and valuable space on the back of the pedicab to local business advertisers. This space can easily generate an additional $500 per month and more in large urban centers. To market your business, be sure to build alliances with hotels, tourist associations, event planners, restaurants, and travel agencies so they can refer your pedicab service to their customers. Additional profits can also be earned by selling commemorative photographs, T-shirts, hats, and postcards. In addition to a local business license, you will also need to purchase general liability insurance. McKay Insurance Agency offers pedicab commercial general liability insurance. They can be contacted at ☎ (641) 842-2135, or online at ☞ www.mckayinsagency.com.

Community Delivery Service

Here is an easy moneymaking opportunity for young people to start. Equipped with nothing more than a cellular telephone to handle incoming and outgoing customer calls, coupled with reliable transportation, you can offer clients in your community fast and convenient delivery and/or pickup services. Pickup and delivery can include dry cleaning, fast foods for lunch, medications, event tickets, groceries, pet foods, flowers, or just about anything else imaginable. The business is also easily expanded simply by putting your marketing and management skills to work concentrating on promoting your community delivery services and securing new customers. Hire your friends with cars to handle the additional pick-ups and deliveries on a revenue-split arrangement. Maximize the efficiency of the operation by installing two-way radios in each vehicle linked to a central dispatcher, thereby limiting down time and non-productive travel time. Of course, you can also keep the business small and do all of the pickups and deliveries yourself, operating nights and weekends only. In addition to advertising with promotional fliers, in the newspaper with cheap classified ads, and with direct mail coupons, also be sure to strike deals with restaurants, grocery stores, pharmacies, and other retailers to handle their delivery services.

Announcement Service

Starting and operating a part-time announcement service is the perfect money-making enterprise for young entrepreneurs who have access to reliable transportation. You can help your clients tell the world about their special occasion or milestone by starting your own yard announcement service. If you are handy with tools and have a creative flair, you can design and build your own special occasion yard announcement cutouts from wood or plastic designed and painted to resemble a stork for birth announcements or a happy birthday caricature, as examples. Or for the non-handyperson, you can purchase predesigned and constructed special occasion cutouts. Customers include any person or business that wants to surprise other people by having announcements placed in their front yards to let everyone in the neighborhood know about the special occasion—birthday, newborn, anniversary, graduation, or for businesses it could mean a sale or a special milestone such as 25 years in business. Depending on the size of the announcement, rental rates are in the range of $30 to $60 per day including delivery and pickup. And you can charge extra by also offering interior and exterior decorating services using balloons, banners, and signs.

Park Cars

What do you need in order to start a special events valet parking service? You will need a valid driver's license, a clean driving record and good parking skills, third-party liability insurance, and an outgoing friendly personality. If you can meet these requirements then you are qualified to start parking cars for big profits. The business can be started with minimal cash and the profit potential is excellent, not to mention that cash tips can really add up. Market your valet parking services to people hosting parties and events, corporations hosting events, and through entertainment industry professionals, such as event and wedding planners, tradeshow organizers, and charity groups and organizations for their special functions. Incredible customer service with a smile will make a favorable impression on customers that is sure to secure lots of repeat business and word-of-mouth referrals. Beyond that there is not much you need to know to successfully operate a valet parking service as this is one of those rare opportunities in which just about everyone of driving age is qualified and has the potential to earn substantial profits. Valet Park, online at ♂ www.valetpark.net, provides lots of helpful information about the valet parking industry.

Mobile RV Wash

Equipment and supplies needed to start a mobile RV wash service add up to nothing more than a stepladder, garden hose, buckets, cleaning and polishing rags, and basic cleaning supplies. Of course, you can invest a little more into equipment such as a power washer and carpet and upholstery cleaner to make your job a little easier and so that you have the ability to offer customers more cleaning options. On that note, offer customers at RV campgrounds detailing and cleaning services such as interior and exterior washing and upholstery steam cleaning. One of the best aspects of this business is the fact that no experience is needed; if you can wash a car, than you can wash an RV. The best way to market RV wash and detailing services is to simply design, print, and distribute promotional fliers describing the various RV detailing services you offer along with rate and contact information. Visit RV parks and campgrounds to hand out the fliers. While you're there also ask park operators if you can place your fliers in the office. Another revenue avenue is to also offer the same interior and exterior cleaning services at mobile home parks.

Rubbish Removal

Hey, cleaning up trash might not be glamorous, but it can earn you excellent part-time profits. The only things you need to start earning money removing trash is a reliable truck, shovels, rakes, gloves, a few garbage cans, and a strong back. You can charge clients by the hour, truckload, or by a quotation before removing their junk. On average, expect to earn in the range of $25 to $40 per hour, after expenses and landfill dumping fees. Providing home and business owners fast and convenient rubbish removal services at competitive prices is the best way to build a reputable business quickly, which will largely be supported by repeat business and word-of-mouth referrals once you are up and running. Also be sure to build alliances with people who can refer your trash removal services to their clients, or become regular customers. These would include real estate agents, residential and commercial cleaners, and home service companies such as carpet cleaners, construction contractors, and residential and commercial property managers. In terms of a low-cost business start-up that requires little in the way of special skills or experience, a rubbish removal service is one of the better choices.

Small-Job Moving Service

Young people with strong backs and a reliable truck can earn as much as $50 per hour offering small-job moving services. You will need to invest a bit of money into equipment such as moving blankets and dollies, but these items are inexpensive if you purchase them secondhand. You can offer both residential and commercial moving services, which can include office and business relocation. Likewise, you can also provide customers with related services such as rubbish removal and delivery services for things such as lumber and furniture to maximize the use of your truck and income potential. Providing clients with additional products such as packing and unpacking services, and selling moving supplies such as cardboard boxes, garment boxes, tape, and bubble wrap will also add bottom line profits. Market your moving and delivery services by running low-cost classified ads in your local newspaper, by creating and delivering promotional fliers describing your service, and by establishing alliances with realtors who can refer your business to their clients. Issues to investigate before you get started include liability insurance and workers' compensation insurance.

Small Sign Installation

If you have access to reliable transportation and you are searching for a simple, part-time, and low-cost business to start that requires no previous experience or special skills, then installing small signs might just fit the bill perfectly. You might be wondering what types of small signs you can easily install. There are lots, including small temporary signs typically used by realtors to advertise a home for sale, politicians to promote their runs for office, and construction companies like painters, roofers, and landscapers who use small site signs to promote the products and services they sell. Generally, these small signs are stuck in the ground in front of homes so that passing motorists and pedestrians will take notice of what is being advertised or promoted. Installing small site signs is very easy and only requires basic tools, such as a sledgehammer and shovel. The profit potential is excellent as rates for providing these types of small sign installation services are currently in the vicinity of $20 for each sign delivered, installed, and removed at a later date. The easiest way to get started is to call on realtors and businesses in your area that typically use small site signs, and pitch the benefits of your service, which should be fast, convenient, reliable, and fairly priced.

Automotive Paint Touch-Up

The future is very bright for a mobile automotive paint touch-up service, especially when you consider that there are more than 130 million vehicles registered in the United States. Bumper scuffs, key scratches, stone chips, and just about every other type of minor automotive paint damage can be quickly and easily fixed at the customer's site using special equipment and color-match paint. In addition to car, truck, van, and motorcycle owners, other potential customers include new and used car dealers, fleet owners, and insurance companies. Don't fret if you do not have paint touch-up experience, because many distributors of mobile automotive painting equipment and products also offer low-cost training workshops that can be completed in less than a few weeks. One such company is Paint Bull, which can be contacted at ☎ (989) 793-2200 or online at ✄ www.paint bull.com. The investment to get started in your own mobile automotive paint touch-up service is reasonable: under $10,000 including equipment, business setup, supplies, and a modest marketing budget, but you will also need or at least have access to, reliable transportation. Extra income can be earned by also providing small dent and ding removal and automotive detailing services.

Bulletin Board Service

Here is a business that just about anyone with a driver's license and access to reliable transportation can start. The business is very simple. In exchange for a flat monthly fee, you post promotional fliers for local retailers, professionals, and service providers on bulletin boards throughout their local trading area. These community bulletin boards are typically found at supermarkets, schools, laundries, libraries, gas stations, community centers, and fitness centers. Most, however, have a policy of removing fliers after one week so that boards do not get overcrowded with outdated information and products for sale, and to allow space for new fliers to be posted. Even though most small business owners realize that posting fliers on community bulletin boards is a fast, frugal, and effective way to advertise their products and services, most do not do it simply because they do not have the time necessary to drive around town posting fliers; they are too busy operating their businesses. This service can be very profitable because you have the potential to post fliers for more than one client at a time. Charge your customers in the range of $20 (not including the cost of the fliers) per week to post their fliers on 50 bulletin boards. This may not seem like a lot of money, but if you have 50 clients, that equals $52,000 a year! And, at only 40 cents per flier posted with the potential of thousands of people stopping to read it, it is lots of exposure for your business customers and a real advertising bargain.

14

WRITING AND PHOTOGRAPHY BUSINESSES

Believe it or not, you can make lots of extra cash writing or taking photographs as you will soon discover. You can work as a freelance writer or photographer, start a video service, publish a community-advertising newsletter, make and sell handmade specialty greeting cards, plus lots more.

Community Advertising Leaflet

Writing, publishing, and distributing a community information and advertising leaflet is a great way to earn extra money. To keep start-up, equipment, and printing costs to a minimum use 11-by-17-inch paper and fold in half as your newspaper. This format will give you four pages in which to feature content in the center and 24 business-card size advertisements around the perimeter. Earn money by selling these advertising spaces to local businesses. If you charge $100 per month for each ad space, you will generate sales of $3,000, of which approximately 20 percent will be needed to cover paper, printing, and distribution costs. The information you feature in the community leaflet can be anything that you think will benefit your readers—entertainment, sports, the arts, or just games and trivia. Deliver the newspaper weekly free of charge to community gathering places such as restaurants, community centers, coffee shops, fitness centers, and transit stations. A computer, software such as Adobe PageMaker, ♂ www.adobe.com, and a printer capable of printing 11-by-17 paper will be needed to operate the business and produce the newspaper. Once you have typeset in all content and advertisements, you can print one copy of the paper and use a local copy shop to complete the run for pennies apiece.

Get Paid to Write

Here is the good news: If you are a wordsmith and love to write, you can make excellent income writing part-time. Here is the bad news: Freelance writing is extremely competitive. In fact, some sources peg the number of freelance writers at 100,000 in the United States alone. Therefore, the majority of successful freelance writers (myself included) will tell you, if you want to make it, you must specialize. Pick a topic that you know, write about it, write about it lots more, and keep on writing about it and submitting your work until you find your voice and a market for your information. You could specialize in youth issues, sports, or entertainment, or if you have specialized knowledge, venture into more specialized niche markets. Freelance writers are typically paid in two ways: either a rate per word or a fixed amount for each story or article. Sometimes further royalties can be earned depending on negotiated republishing rights. To get the ballpoint pen rolling and some publishing credits, expect to write a few freebies in order to get your name out. The best paying markets tend to be major monthly magazines, newspapers, and journals. The least attractive pay is usually for content for web publishing. There are a number of web sites chockful of helpful information to get freelance writers on their way to earning big profits, such as Absolute Write, ♂ www .absolutewrite.com.

Calligraphic Services

Turn your talent for exquisite handwriting into a profitable business by providing customers with calligraphy services and selling calligraphy products. Even young people with minimal artistic ability can easily learn to master the art of calligraphy. How? Because there are numerous books like 📖 *The Calligrapher's Bible: 100 Complete Alphabets and How to Draw Them* by David Harris (Barron's, 2003), as well as kits available that can help you master the craft with practice. Calligraphy can be used to create one-of-a-kind handwritten wedding and event invitations, restaurant menus, gift basket cards, classy product labels, business cards, award certificates, greeting cards, thank-you cards, stationery, and to design business and club logos. Likewise, print shops and stationery retailers are often asked for special designs requiring calligraphy; because the majority only offer machine-printed calligraphy, there is a great opportunity to subcontract your services to fill to this void in the marketplace. Be sure to create a portfolio of work that can be distributed to wedding consultants, restaurants, banquet facilities, associations, and clubs throughout your community, as well as print and stationery shops. This is a low-cost business to get started right from mom and dad's kitchen table, and rates are in the range of $25 to $50 per hour. Lots of information can be found about calligraphy by visiting Calligraphy Centre, ✂ www.calligraphycentre.com, and the Society for Calligraphy, ✂ www.societyforcalligraphy.com.

Print and Electronic Newsletter Service

By making use of your research, writing, and design skills, you can create informative print and/or electronic promotional newsletters to meet your client's specific wants and needs. These potential clients can include stockbrokers, realtors, small business owners, service providers, sports clubs, nonprofit organizations, and corporations. Even though most organizations and businesses realize the benefits of newsletters, like keeping clients and members informed about the latest news, and promoting products and services, many do not have the skills, time, or people power to get the job done on a regular basis. Writing, designing, printing, and distributing print and electronic newsletters will require an investment into computer hardware, software, and related equipment such as a scanner, laser printer, and digital camera, but at $25 to $40 per hour, the return on investment is quick. Create print and electronic newsletter samples to use as your main marketing tools. Print samples can be mailed and hand delivered to potential clients, while e-newsletters can be delivered by e-mail. Networking at business functions and talking to small business owners will also go a long way in spreading the word about the services you offer. Check out 📖 *Design It Yourself Newsletters: A Step-by-Step Guide* by Chuck Green (Rockport Publishers, 2002), a helpful book full of great tips, and E-Newsletter Pro, ✂ www.enewsletterpro.com, sells newsletter management software.

Resume Service

Young wordsmiths take notice: Big bucks can be earned creating resumes for the millions of people in search of employment every year. Finding the perfect words to describe why you should get the job and not someone else is difficult, and that is one reason why resume services continue to flourish in spite of the fact that just about everybody has access to a computer and a word processing program. One of the best aspects about selling resume services is you can work from home or your dorm room and keep start-up costs to a minimum, making this the perfect opportunity for young people looking to earn an extra few hundred dollars every month. In addition to creating resumes, writing cover, sales, and follow-up letters for customers can increase revenues. Advertise locally, online, and through career exposition trade shows. Once established, this is the type of business supported mainly through word-of-mouth advertising and repeat business. Win Way, located online at ♂ www.winway.com, has custom resume writing software applications available. Additionally, an excellent book on the subject of writing resumes is 📖 *The Resume Handbook: How to Write Outstanding Resumes & Cover Letters for Every Situation* by Arthur D. Rosenberg and David Heizer (Adams Media Corporation, 2003). This book is packed full of helpful advice and information.

Produce Personalized Story Books

Crating and selling personalized story time books is a fantastic part-time money-making opportunity for entrepreneurial young adults. Every child loves a good story and the market for personalized storybooks for kids is gigantic. What makes creating personalized storybooks so unique is that each customer's child (or children) becomes the main character in the story, and friends and family members are often supporting characters. Software applications are available from companies like Create-A-Book, ♂ www.hefty.com, and My Family Tales, ♂ www.myfamilytales.com, with story reprint rights that make this business a snap. Basically change the names of the characters to suit, print, and sell. Alternately, if you are a wordsmith, you can create your own story lines changing the names of the characters to those of your customer's children. To operate the business you will need a computer, a good quality printer, and a digital camera if you are going to include images of the children in your stories. In addition to creating personalized story books for friends, family, and neighbors, you can also set up at malls, flea markets, craft shows, and community events on weekends and during the summer to offer clients personalized storybooks while they wait.

Handcrafted Greeting Cards

A very exciting and potentially lucrative moneymaking opportunity awaits enterprising young entrepreneurs who have the skills needed to design, produce, and sell handcrafted greeting cards. One idea is to go after the high-end greeting card market and paint original watercolor scenes to suit occasions such as seasonal holidays and milestone events on blank greeting card stock, or by hiring local artists to do the artwork if you do not have artistic talent, effectively making each card a highly collectible piece of artwork. Or cards can be completed with generic paintings and text. They can then be sold through retailers on a wholesale or consignment basis, direct to businesses for promotional activities, and directly to consumers via mall sales kiosks, eBay, and by establishing alliances with wedding and event planners who can refer your one-of-a-kind artist cards to their clients. Likewise, you could also concentrate on only business-to-business sales by customizing each greeting card to each business. A couple of great books on the subject include 📖 *Designing Handcrafted Cards: Step-by-Step Techniques for Crafting 60 Beautiful Cards* by Claire Sun-Ok Choi (Quarry Books, 2004), and 📖 *Making Greeting Cards with Creative Materials* by Mary Jo McGraw (David & Charles Publishers, 2002).

Family Tree Research Service

Many people have a keen interest in finding out more about their families and ancestral pasts, especially if the research reveals past royal connections or connections with characters of dubious distinction or notoriety. Technology, and more importantly the internet, has made a family tree research service not only an easy business to start for young people, but also a business that can connect you with potential clients worldwide. The premise is really quite simple; clients pay you a fee for researching information about their family trees. The information you find can then be compiled into an orderly "family tree" and presented to your client. The income potential for providing this type of service is excellent, in the range of $15 to $20 per hour. Advertise your service locally utilizing promotional fliers and word-of-mouth referral, as well as online by posting messages in forums related to family genealogy. This is a great business for young people because the investment needed to get started is almost zero if you already have a computer and internet access, and because almost all of your work can be done online, on the telephone, or in libraries, you can work from just about anywhere.

Photography

If you would love to make extra money snapping and selling photographs, you'll be happy to know that you can! The internet has breathed new life into the freelance photography industry, mainly because it is now very easy to send pictures to publishers, editors, copywriters, marketers, and designers all around the globe in a matter of moments using email. Not to mention that billions of photographic images are needed to fill the now more than four billion (and climbing) web pages. In addition to the internet, there are also millions of print publications, media companies, retailers, marketers, organizations, government agencies, and more who need new photographs every single day to add meaning to newspapers, newsletters, magazines, brochures, catalogs, and presentations. Needless to say, young people with photographic skills and a bit of marketing savvy have the opportunity to earn lots of cash taking and selling photographs. You can contract with publishers and others needing photographic images directly, or post your photos on any one of the many stock photography services online, such as Photos To Go, ♂ www.photostogo.com, and Photo Search, ♂ www.photosearch.com. On these sites, people browse the selection and purchase photographic images that they need. You are paid a one-time fee, or a royalty, each time the image is downloaded, depending on your agreement with the image broker. Books such as 📖 2006 *Photographer's Market* by Donna Poehner (Writer's Digest Books, 2005) are excellent resources packed with information about where you can sell you photographs and who you need to contact. The International Freelance Photographers Organization located online at ♂ www.aipress.com also provides lots of helpful information and resources for the aspiring freelance photographer.

Pet Photography

As an animal lover, I cannot image a business that would be more fun and rewarding than operating a pet photography service. Unfortunately, I am not a very good photographer, but if you are and you love pets, then what are you waiting for, start a part-time pet photography service. Operating on a mobile basis, you can visit owners of dogs, cats, reptiles, horses, champion livestock, birds, and even fish to take the photographs. Making the experience fun for pets and their owners will also go a long way to secure repeat business and a ton of referrals, so liven things up with pet costumes, themed backdrops, and by offering pet videotaping services as well, complete with music, titles, and special effects. Likewise, to boost profit potential, also offer a wide assortment of products that customers can have their pets' photographic images transferred onto—key tags, greeting cards, calendars, mugs, hats, T-shirts, sports bags, and bumper stickers.

Portrait Photography

Calling all young entrepreneurial hobby photographers! Why not profit from your skills by starting a portrait photography service? Much like pet photography, you can work part-time and operate on a mobile basis going to your client's home, office, or business. Also like pet photography, you can easily increase profits by simply offering to place the photographic images you take on a wide variety of products including greeting cards, calendars, mugs, and T-shirts. Promote the business by utilizing print advertising media such as fliers and classified newspaper ads, as well as by working with local shop owners who will allow you to set up weekend portrait studios in their locations on revenue split basis. Also do not overlook sports clubs, charity organizations, social clubs, and corporations as potential clients, as most put together an annual yearbook featuring employee, member, or volunteer's photographs.

Construction Photography

Capitalizing on your basic photography skills you can start a construction photography service. Each year thousands of new homes and apartments are built, and a construction photography service provides new homeowners with a complete photo album of the construction, right from the hole in the ground to the moment the moving truck arrives. The photography service can be provided both in traditional film format as well as digital format utilizing a digital camera. However, do not waste your time chasing down the individual who is building a new home. Instead, go after homebuilders and property developers, because many of these companies build hundreds of new homes each year. Not only will securing photography contracts with these companies generate a handsome profit for you, it is also goodwill and a great marketing tool for the construction company. Imagine once the new house is completed, the owner or manager of the construction company presents the new homeowners with a complete photo album or CD-ROM chronicling the home's construction from start to finish.

CHAPTER

15

SERVICE-RELATED BUSINESSES

The best aspect about providing a service in exchange for a fee is that everyone is qualified. Everyone has a skill, knowledge, or experience that other people are willing to pay for in the form of a service that you provide, for you to teach them your specific skill or knowledge. The trick is, of course, to identify the skills you do have that can be sold in the form of providing a service. Any skill that you have is your best and most marketable asset. For instance, if know how to paint, then people will pay you to paint their houses. If you are skilled at arranging flowers, they will pay for that. However, most people have a tendency to underestimate the true value of their skill sets and experiences. You have to remember, what may come naturally to you may not come so naturally to others. Likewise, you might think that your particular knowledge or expertise may be of little value, but if someone else needs or wants to learn about that knowledge it is very valuable to them. In this chapter you will find many services that you can provide for a profit. Maybe one is right for you!

Get Paid to Wait

How are you going to spend your summer vacation? If you're smart you'll spend it by starting a waiting service—get paid to do nothing more than wait around! What exactly is a waiting service? You charge people a fee to stay at their home and wait to accept a delivery, to let in a plumber or electrician, to wait for the telephone or cable company, to wait for a furniture delivery, or any other number of reasons. Waiting services are really starting to become very popular because most working people cannot afford to sit around all day waiting for a delivery or the repairman. The costs to start this business are very low. You will need to spend a bit for marketing materials like fliers and business cards, but that's about it. You can charge customers $5 to $10 per hour for this service. Promote the service by establishing alliances with companies that typically require people to wait, such as the telephone company, plumbers, electricians, cable television companies, and courier companies. That way the next time one of their customers tries to pin them down to an exact time, they can simply refer your service. If you are really ambitious, you can even earn more money by hiring your friends to also wait at peoples' homes and keep a small percentage of the money they earn. And while you are waiting, you can be working on fliers or sales letters for one of your other businesses!

Sewing Skills

Calling all young people with sewing skills and a sewing machine! It's time to cash in on your sewing skills by providing garment and fabric alteration services right from your home or dorm room and earn a bundle of extra money in the process. Dry cleaners, fashion retailers, uniform retailers, bridal boutiques, costume shops, drapery studios, and consignment clothing shops—all are potential customers for your service. In fact, any businesses that retail or rent clothing of any sort are potential customers. For that matter, so is any person who is in need of alteration services. Perhaps the easiest way to get started is to put on a comfortable pair of shoes and start calling on the aforementioned businesses that are most likely to require alteration services. To sweeten the deal, providing you have access to reliable transportation or public transit, offer free pick-up and delivery, fast turnaround times, great service, and quality workmanship, all at fair prices. Your business clients benefit because they can offer alteration services to customers for free, ensuring repeat business. Or, they can also profit by marking up what you charge. Along your sewing skills, you will need the tools of the sewing trade. Online companies like Bright Notions, ♂ www.brightnotions.com, and Sew True, ♂ www.sewtrue.com, sell sewing equipment and supplies at discount prices.

Personal Shopper

Calling all young adults that love to shop, this is the opportunity for you. Earn great money and have fun by starting a personal shopping service assisting people who are too busy to shop, who don't like to shop, or who can't get out to shop, and get paid to do their shopping for them. Shop for things like clothing, furniture, and electronics. And lots of busy people hire personal shoppers to select gifts for any number of special occasions, including birthdays, births, weddings, Christmas, and anniversaries. Personal shoppers are also hired by interior designers and collectors to rummage through flea markets, consignment shops, antique shops, and garage sales for collectibles, art, books, antiques, and funky home and office decor items. Corporations hire personal shoppers to purchase perfect gifts for customers, employees, and executives, as well as to purchase products for gift bag giveaways at events, ceremonies, and seminars. Seniors and other people who may find it difficult, or who can't get out of their homes, hire personal shoppers to purchase groceries, clothing, and other home and personal products. Best of all, no experience is required to get started. If you love to shop, are creative, and don't mind networking with business owners, corporate executives, and people from all walks of life, you're qualified to become a personal shopper.

Holiday and Event Decorating

One of the hottest new services to sell is holiday and event decoration services. Not only is there the potential to earn big bucks and have a lot of fun doing it, but the business is also perfect for young people because start-up costs and experience are minimal. Holiday and event decorators offer clients a wide variety or services—everything from installing Christmas lights, to decorating banquet halls for wedding receptions, to "creeping-out" a house, business, or office for Halloween celebrations. In other words you can let your imagination run wild. In addition to Christmas and special occasions you can also help decorate customers' homes, stores, and offices for milestones celebrations such as anniversaries or Halloween, Easter, New Year's, and Fourth of July celebrations. To provide clients with holiday and special event decorating services you will need basic tools like ladders, a cordless drill, and hand tools, along with a flair for creative design and suitable transportation. Decorations may be purchased wholesale and marked up for retail providing an additional revenue source. Ultimately, your work decorating will be your greatest advertisement, so be sure to use site signs promoting your service, hand out lots of business cards and fliers, and send out press releases to the media when you have really done a bang-up decorating job on a business, house, or office.

House Sitting

There are lots of people who regularly or just occasionally need house sitting services, including people going on vacations lasting longer than a week, and traveling business owners and executives, just to name a few. House sitting provides an excellent opportunity for young people to earn extra cash because the service is easy to market, demand is proven, and the business is cheap to start. House sitters not only provide peace of mind security, but they also provide clients with other valuable services while on the job, such as watering plants and the lawn, feeding the cat, collecting mail, house cleaning duties, and taking care of any emergency situations that may arise, such as calling a plumber if a water pipe bursts. You have a couple of options in terms of how you establish a housesitting service. Rates vary depending on the length of the job, as well as additional services that homeowners may require, but you can charge at least $10 per hour. Some housesitting jobs will require you to stay overnight, while others may only require you to check in on the home before and after school. Increasing revenues can be as easy as adding additional, but complementary, services like pet sitting, dog walking, and baby-sitting. House Sit World located online at ♂ www.house sitworld.com provides lots of helpful information about house sitting.

Painting Houses

Interior and exterior residential house painting is a great moneymaking opportunity for young people who are not afraid to roll up their sleeves and get to work. Even better, starting and operating a painting service is perfectly suited to young people because unlike a lot of other home improvement businesses that require a great deal of skill, just about everyone can paint—and you only get better with practice. Of course, key to success in this business is to provide clients with uncompromising quality and service, which in turn helps to secure more repeat and referral business. You can market your painting services by designing a promotional flier outlining the details along with contact information and distribute these to homes in your area. In addition to reliable transportation, you will also need to invest a small amount of money into purchasing tools and equipment such as an extension ladder, stepladder, scrapers, sanding blocks, rollers and trays, brushes, and drop cloths. In total, expect to invest about $500 into the required tools. But don't worry because return on your investment can be quick and very profitable, as you will be able to charge between $15 and $30 per hour for painting services.

Packing

The hardest part of moving is packing because it can be slow, tedious, and back-breaking work. These same reasons are what make starting a packing service such a great idea, especially if you are a young person with a strong back and are not afraid of a little hard work. Moving companies specializing in both residential and office moving will be your main source of work because they can subcontract your service or refer your service to their customers. Finding moving companies to work for is easy: Simply pick up your local telephone directories and look under "Movers." You can also visit web sites such as The American Moving and Storage Association, ♂ www.moving.org, and The Canadian Association of Movers, ♂ www.mover.net, to find moving companies in your area. You can also run low-cost classified advertisements in your local newspaper under the "Moving" heading, and post fliers on bulletin boards throughout the community to get the telephone ringing. You can charge about $10 to $12 per hour for your packing services and hire friends to help out when you are really busy. Outside of reliable transportation to get to jobs, nothing else is needed to start.

Assemble Products

Furniture, lawn and garden products, fitness equipment, and computers, all require assembly, which is never as easy as advertised. Opportunity is always born out of circumstance. In this case that means there is a fantastic opportunity to offer product assembly services and earn a great part-time income in the process. Even better, getting your own product assembly service off the ground costs well under $500, excluding transportation. Market your product assembly services through retailers who do not currently offer product assembly services to their customers; you can also earn extra money if you can deliver the product as well. You will need to buy basic tools such as a cordless drill, hand tools, and a socket set, along with moving equipment like blankets and a dolly, and suitable transportation if you will also be offering delivery services. Retailers of products that must be assembled after purchase will be your big market, but at the same time do not overlook the possibility of building alliances with home and office movers; moving often requires furniture and equipment to be disassembled for the move and reassembled after the move.

Nonmedical Home Care Services

Very responsible young people can earn an excellent part-time wage providing nonmedical home care services for seniors and people with disabilities. One reason that nonmedical home care is an exploding industry is our aging population. People over 50 is the fastest expanding group in North America, and as a general rule as people age they tend to need more personal attention. Nonmedical home care services provide clients with a wide range of services specific to each individual's needs. These services can include companionship, meal preparation, medication reminders, light housekeeping duties, laundry, running errands, trips to appointments, shopping for groceries, and other personal needs. As mentioned, in addition to seniors, nonmedical home care workers also provide similar services for new moms, people with disabilities, and people recovering from injury or illness. If you are responsible, reliable, compassionate, and care about the welfare of others, you can thrive in this business and earn a part-time wage in the area of $12 to $15 per hour working before and after school and on weekends. Market your services by running low-cost classified advertisements in your local newspaper, and also by talking with doctors and explaining the services you provide, as they can refer their patients to your business.

Glass Etching

You can do glass etching from home and strike it rich! Glass etching is a great moneymaking opportunity for may reasons, but mainly because glass etching is quick to learn, equipment and supplies are inexpensive, and demand for decorative etched glass is proven. There are a few techniques that can be used to decoratively etch glass—acid wash, engraving, laser etching, and sandblasting. At present, sandblasting remains the most popular choice and this method is accomplished by covering the glass with a stencil pattern and blowing sand against the surface, and glass surfaces that are not protected by the pattern becomes etched. Products that can be etched with eloquent designs, patterns, and images for resale include window glass, cabinet glass, glass awards, glass tables, signs on door and window glass, automotive glass, mirrors, glassware, and sun catchers, as well as etching glass with codes and identification marks for security purposes. There are many ready-made etching stencil designs and letter stencils available through crafts retailers or you can make your own by purchasing, stenciling vinyl, and cutting your own patterns. In addition to selling etched glass products online and at home décor shows, you can also do custom one-of-a-kind glass etching work for interior designers, kitchen cabinet installers, and automotive dealers. ▢ *Easy Glass Etching* by Marlis Cornett (Sterling, 2004), provides helpful information about glass etching, and Martronics Corporation located online at ♂ www.glass-etching-kits .com, sells glass etching tools and supplies.

Temp Help Agency

Supplying temporary workers is a thriving industry, and you can cash in by starting your own temp help service. In short, when businesses and organizations need temporary or seasonal help, many utilize the services of a temporary help agency to fulfill their peoplepower needs, rather than having to run help wanted ads and interview potential candidates. This is because it is often cheaper and always more convenient to use the services of a temp agency. For young entrepreneurs I would suggest that you specialize in running a temporary help agency for young people. Recruiting young people prepared to work on a temporary basis should not prove difficult, mainly because every young person is looking to earn extra or occasional money, especially during summer months. Marketing can be as easy as creating an information package describing the service and your available workforce and distributing the packages to businesses that occasionally rely on temporary workers, as well as networking for clients at business and social functions, and by running newspaper classified ads. The accounting side of the business is very basic. You hire out your workers at a fixed rate, which will vary depending the type of work they are doing, and retain a portion of their income. For instance, you might hire out farm helpers at $12 per hour, pay the worker $10 per hour and retain a $2 per hour fee. Keeping in mind you will need to do all administrative work, issue checks, and collect and remit income taxes and worker compensation fees.

Babysitting Referral Service

Take heart in the fact that there are three ways to earn great money running a babysitting referral service. The first is to charge babysitters a fee to join your referral service, be listed in the directory, and have access to parents seeking babysitting services. The second option is to charge parents a fee to join the service; this will entitle them to have access to the babysitters' directory to find a suitable and qualified babysitter in their area. And the third way to earn money is to sell advertising space on your web site and in your monthly "Babysitting Newsletter" to local children- and baby-related businesses that want to advertise to your customer base. All three options have the potential to generate huge profits for the innovative young entrepreneur with strong marketing and management skills. Best of all you can work from home or your dorm room and have parents and babysitters sign up and pay for services online. Of course, it will be important to develop a screening system for both potential babysitters, as well as parents looking for babysitters, to offer both peace of mind in terms of qualifications, suitability, and security. It is also a good idea to insist that all babysitters have basic first aid training, as well as be bonded to provide parents with an additional layer of protection.

Floral Design

Flowers are big business. In fact, the floral industry in the United States generates a whopping $20 billion a year in sales! If you love flowers, have an eye for design, and would like to earn some extra part-time cash, then you are qualified to start your own floral design business. Floral design training is an asset, and there are a number of schools and community continuing education programs that offer floral design classes, but once again, you can teach yourself the basics and master the craft with practice on the job. A good book chockful of helpful tips is 📖 *Flowers: The Complete Book of Floral Design* by Paula Pryke (Rizzoli, 2004). In a nutshell, floral designers select flowers, greenery, and decorations to be used to create appealing floral arrangements such as bouquets, wreaths, and table centerpieces for any number of occasions—weddings, funerals, social events, restaurants, and business functions. Designers also use a variety of tools and materials, such as various knives and shears to produce the desired cut and shape, as well as foam, wire, tape, and all kinds of containers to hold and showcase their designs. Market your services by contacting event planners, wedding planners, restaurants, catering companies, and funeral homes to discuss your designs and offer your services.

Run Errands

Let's face it, today's busy lifestyles means that many working folk do not have time for even the simplest of errands. Which is great news if you're a multitasker looking to start your own simple, inexpensive, yet potentially very profitable part-time business. An errand service doing things like picking up groceries or taking the family pet to the veterinarian for a routine checkup can be operated with nothing more than a cellular telephone and reliable transportation. Land clients by creating a simple marketing brochure explaining the services you provide along with your contact information. The brochures can be pinned to community bulletin boards, hand delivered to homes and businesses, and distributed with the local newspaper. A few promotional items such as pens and memo pads emblazoned with your business logo, name, and telephone number given out to current and potential customers will go a long way as a gentle reminder of your fast, reliable, and affordable errand services. This is the kind of business where growth is fuelled by referrals, so customer service and satisfaction are the most important goals. Expanding the business to include fast food delivery services will also help add substantial income and profits.

Conducting Garage and Estate Sales

Weekend profits await young entrepreneurs with good marketing and organizational skills who become garage and estate sale promoters. Garage, lawn, and estate sales are hugely popular events in every community across North America. In fact, it is estimated that more than 60 million people go garage sale shopping annually, generating billions of dollars in sales. As a promoter, you can provide clients who do not have the time or gumption to hold their own sales, with the service of organizing and conducting the sale for them. Your duties will include promoting, organizing, selling items, and cleaning up after everyone has gone home. In exchange for providing this valuable service, you retain a percentage of the total sales. I would suggest 25 percent for larger sales and up to 50 percent for smaller sales. Once you have secured a client, be sure to canvas the immediate neighborhood and solicit for additional items to be placed in the sale on consignment. Why hold a small sale if you can increase sales and profits by enlisting neighbors to provide items, too? Promote the sales with professional site signage and in community newspapers that do not charge for small classified ads or for garage sale listings.

Cloth Diaper Service

Disposable diapers often irritate a baby's skin. A solution is environmentally friendly cloth diapers made of natural fibers, which are soft to the baby's skin and can be cleaned and reused many times. A baby can go through as many as 4,000 diapers before being fully potty trained. So you do not have to be a genius to figure out that an outstanding business opportunity awaits ambitious young entrepreneurs who start a cloth diaper delivery service. You can offer a complete service, including diaper supply, delivery, pickup, and cleaning. If mom and dad don't mind, you can clean the diapers at home using your laundry equipment, or have a established commercial laundry clean the diapers at a discount rate for volume. Word-of-mouth marketing will be your main promotional tool, so be sure to get out and start the promotional train rolling by talking with as many new parents as you can. Diaper Pin, located online at ♂ www.diaper pin.com, and Worldwide Diapering Resource, located online at ♂ www.born tolove.com, both provide lots of helpful cloth diaper information, links, and resources.

Greeting Card Service

The majority of small business owners and salespeople know that one of the keys to successful customer retention is regular contact. But at the same time, many are so busy working 60 hours a week, it leaves little time to even send a simple "thank you," "thinking of you," or "congratulations on this special day" greeting card. By starting a greeting card service you will be able to help your business clients stay in regular contact with all of their clients. You will need to build a database and create files for all clients. Each client file should include full contact information for their customers including telephone, email, and mailing address, as well as more specific information such as birthdays and anniversaries. Having this information will enable you to automatically send your client's customers greeting cards regularly—Christmas, birthdays, Fourth of July, and to announce special sales or other information that your clients want to periodically include. Additionally, you should work with a graphic designer and print shop so that each greeting card can be specific to each of your client's businesses. Ideal candidates for a greeting card service include car dealers, realtors, corporations, associations, and clubs that would like to send to members, lawyers, accountants, and doctors. Rates will vary depending on the quantity of cards sent for each client, frequency of cards sent, as well as each client's greeting card design and selection.

Public Opinion and Focus Group Service

From the smallest Mom and Pop businesses to the largest international corporations, businesses often rely on public opinion surveys and focus groups to learn more about their products, services, competition, and customers. Of course, starting and operating a public opinion and focus group service is generally something that businesspeople with lots of experience and education would do, but so can you even without experience. In fact, you might even have an advantage because your perspective will be that of a younger person, which is a demographic that most businesses are really trying to tap in to. Public opinion polls and surveys can be conducted on the telephone, by mail, e-mail, web site polling, or by way of personal interview. Focus groups are comprised of people who meet your client's demographic; they are asked what they think about a product or service, in many cases based on trying the product or service. To get started, create and conduct a few of your own public opinion polls on topics that would be interesting to the public at large, again focusing on young people, such as how young people rate various fashion brands, or movies, and so forth. Send local media the results in the form of a press release or media alert, and use the media coverage of your polls and surveys as a marketing tool to secure paying customers, small businesses, and corporations for the service.

Babysitting

For decades babysitting has been a steadfast way for young adults to earn extra money. Many parents find it very difficult to find dependable babysitters. So if you are reliable and do a good job, you can be guaranteed babysitting work for many years, and a ton of referral business when your customers start telling their friends about you. Surprisingly enough babysitting can also really pay off, especially during peak holiday times such as New Year's and Christmas when you can easily charge $15 per hour. You can even charge more if you are willing to also do light housekeeping duties such as laundry and cleaning. Start in your own neighborhood and deliver fliers promoting your service; it will probably only take a day or two for the calls from eager parents to start rolling in. I would also suggest that you take a first aid training course, as this will make a positive impression on nervous parents and give you the ability to handle an emergency should it happen.

New Parent Helper

Let's face it: parents with newborns need all the help they can get—looking after the baby, cleaning, cooking, and picking up groceries. This in turn creates a fantastic opportunity for young people to start a new parent helper service providing these services and lots more. This business is more involved than just babysitting. In most instances, parents are home and require help with day-to-day chores in addition to looking after the new baby, especially if they are adjusting to life with their first child. Marketing the service is as easy as creating a flier describing the services you provide for new parents and delivering the flier to homes in your community, as well as posting them on notice boards. It won't take long until your telephone is ringing off the hook and you have a line of overwhelmed busy new parents ready to jump at the chance to get help around the home. On average you should have no problem charging in the range of $8 to $12 per hour for the service, which makes this the perfect opportunity for young people who want to earn a bit of extra money after school and on weekends.

Garage and Basement Organizer

Big bucks can be earned by young people of all ages by cleaning up and organizing garages and basements. To start your own garage and basement organizer service requires no special skills or equipment other than some basic hand tools and a strong back. Ideally, you can start close to home by providing the service to family, friends, and neighbors while you build a strong referral base. The business does not need much description other than to say that your main duties will be to clean up and organize these areas. You can charge by the job providing an estimate first, or charge a flat hourly rate, which should be in the range of $8 to $12 per hour. You will need to invest a bit of money into brooms, garbage cans, and possibly a shop vac, but outside of that and basic business cards, there are no additional costs to getting started.

Student Housing Service

Finding suitable and affordable living accommodations is very difficult for most college and university students, especially if they cannot arrange dorm or campus housing. While there are many sources of information in regards to apartments for rent for students, this opportunity focuses on locating room-and-board accommodations for students. Many homeowners living in close proximity to colleges and universities have space to accommodate students in a room-and-board situation. This venture simply provides the service of bringing these two parties together. The business can easily be operated as an online enterprise. Therefore, you will need to develop a web site enabling homeowners to post student rooms for rent, as well as a separate category for students to post their accommodation needs.

Income is earned by charging the students and landlords a small fee, in the range of $20 to $25 each, for providing this very valuable student housing service. To generate initial listings and help build the business, offer free listings for a trial period of a month or so. This should help to secure listings and generate hits on the site.

Install Security Peepholes

Calling all cash-starved university and high school students! If you are looking to start a simple business on a limited budget, and that has excellent part-time income potential, than look no further than starting a peephole installation service. Millions of homes and apartments have older-style doors that do not have security peepholes. This means there are millions of potential customers just waiting for you to install a peephole. Selling the service is easy: Simply start knocking on doors without security peepholes and explain the security benefits of a peephole to the residents of the home. The peepholes are easy to install and generally take less than ten minutes to complete. There are no regulations to comply with, and the equipment needed for the installations amounts to no more than a cordless drill and a few drill bits. Peepholes can be purchased for less than $3 each, and the income potential is outstanding, as you can easily charge $20 to $25 for each peephole installed.

Welcome New People to the Neighborhood

Here is a great moneymaking enterprise that requires no practical business experience, and very little investment to start, which makes it the perfect opportunity for just about any young person. A welcome wagon service is simply making new residents of your community feel welcome and explaining all the various services and attractions that are available locally, including parks, schools, restaurants, hospitals, government agencies, and such. Local businesses pay you a small fee in exchange for promoting their products and services to new residents, thus creating income. Generally this would include promotional coupons, a free product or service, or some other sort of promotion to attract the new residents to the participating businesses. These small fees really start to add up, especially if you are promoting 30 to 40 local businesses at any one time. To get information about new arrivals in your community, build alliances with real estate agents, business associations, and schools. And to market your service create an information package describing the benefit of your service and distribute it to local retailers and service providers.

Coin Search

Coin searching is an excellent moneymaking venture that requires absolutely no selling, advertising, managing, or record keeping. Does this sound too good to be true? Well, it is true. Coin searching can earn you a ton of profits in your spare time and few young people even know about this moneymaking secret. Here's how it works: Simply start with $100 (or less if you want), go to your local bank, and purchase $100 worth of rolled coins. The rest is easy. Once you are home, break apart the rolls and start searching for valuable coins that have unknowingly been rolled with the rest of the coins. Keep the valuable coins for resale, reroll the leftover coins, and start the process over again with new coin rolls. It's just that simple. Of course, you will need to educate yourself about coins. This can be accomplished by studying price guides such as 📖 *The Official Blackbook Price Guide to U.S. Coins* by Marc Hudgeons and Thomas Hudgeons (House of Collectables, 2005). That way if you happen to find a 1937-D 3-legged buffalo error nickel in one of the rolls you'll know that you have found a coin that is worth about $150.

Professional Greeter

Thanks to Wal-Mart an entirely new part-time flexible profession has been created, which is the professional greeter. Wal-Mart pioneered and perfected using greeters at their stores to make shoppers feel welcome and part of the community, and this approach has worked with great success. Now many other retailers, corporations, and organizations have learned from this example and have jumped on the bandwagon also employing professional greeters to make customers and guests feel welcome and part of the family. Starting a freelance professional greeter service is an excellent moneymaking opportunity for young people because there are few requirements to get started; if you are personable, like to smile, and like to help people even more, then you are qualified to be a professional greeter. In addition to department stores, retailers such as car dealers, building supply retailers, restaurants, garden centers, RV parks, corporations, charitable events, and casinos enlist the services of professional greeters. This is very much a business that is built one step at a time because it will take time to develop a reputation and a solid customer base. But with that said, the investment to get started is virtually zero, as are the operating overheads, yet you can charge anywhere up to $25 per hour for your services and have the flexibility of working full-time in the summer months and part-time during school months.

Creating Window Displays

Retailers need attention-grabbing window displays to draw customers into their shops, but not all retailers have the time it takes to create window displays that will get the job done. Starting a business specializing in creating effective window merchandise displays for retailers is the focus of this opportunity. Young people with creative minds will be well suited to take up the challenge and have the potential to cash in for big profits. To market the service, set appointments with local retailers and explain that window space is one of the best and least expensive marketing tools they have available; a 24-hour silent salesperson. Window space can be used to display new products, demonstrate products, and motivate impulse buying. In short, well-planned and well-executed window displays increase revenues and profits. In addition to an artistic flair, you will need to build an inventory of interesting props, signs, and lighting options. Remember, your goal is not a one-time sale, but to return weekly, biweekly, or monthly to create new window displays for every customer.

16

CLEANING SERVICE BUSINESSES

If you're like me and don't like dirt, grime, or clutter, then starting a cleaning service will be the perfect way for you to earn lots of extra money. Cleaning-related businesses are proven winners that take little in the way of start-up cash or experience to get rolling. This makes them perfect candidates as new business ventures for motivated young entrepreneurs that don't mind rolling up their sleeves and getting to work. There are also many types of cleaning services that you can pursue—residential, automotive, office, window washing, or even a simple laundry service. These, and many more are all featured in this chapter.

Litter Pick-Up

Calling younger folks of all ages! If you are looking for an easy business to start that requires no special skills or experience, and a start-up investment of only a few hundred dollars, yet still has excellent income potential, a litter pickup service might be just what you have been searching for. Armed with nothing more than the basic tools of the trade such as a rake, shovel, garbage can, and a pair of gloves, you can quickly be cleaning up litter for paying customers in your community. Call on retailers, professionals, and other business owners who need to project a good business image, because having litter in and around their businesses in parking lots, lawns, flowerbeds, and sidewalks is not the positive image they want to project. Design and produce a promotional flier outlining your service and how much you charge and hand deliver the fliers to retailers and other businesses with storefronts and parking lots. In exchange for a flat monthly fee of say $50, you can visit your customer's business locations daily and pick up any litter within close proximity to their shops—sidewalks, entrances, flowerbeds, lawns, and parking lots. It won't take long for word to spread and in no time you will probably have more part-time work than you can handle.

Power Washing

There are literally hundreds of things that can be cleaned using power-washing equipment including driveways, patios, parking lots, recreational vehicles, mobile homes, cars, boats, store signs, awnings, metal roofs, trailers, and construction and farm equipment. Not only is there a nearly unlimited number of items to pressure wash, you can earn big bucks cleaning them because power-washing rates start at about $30 per hour; it is not uncommon to earn as much as $400 per day power washing once you have built a reputation for reliability and quality work. The fixed costs associated with operating the service are a telephone, liability insurance, transportation, the occasional equipment repair, and a bit of initial advertising until repeat business and referrals kick in and make up the lion's share of your work. A helpful hint to keep in mind when you start marketing is to aim your efforts at clients that will become repeat clients. These include companies with fleet vehicles and retailers who want to keep their storefronts and parking lots spic-n-span. The reason you want to target repeat business is that it costs 100 times as much to find 100 clients as opposed to finding one client and servicing them

100 times. You can also visit marinas, trailer parks, and RV campgrounds on weekends and offer your pressure-washing services to boat, trailer, and recreational vehicle owners at reduced rates because you can make up the difference (and more) through volume power washing. E-Power Wash located online at ☞ www.epower wash.com has lots of helpful information about starting and operating a power-washing service.

Laundry Service

Starting and operating a laundry wash-and-fold service might not be glamorous, but it can be a great way for young people to earn extra cash. Even better, assuming you already have access to a washer and dryer, the investment needed to start and clean laundry from home adds up to nothing more than a few hundred dollars to cover the cost of business cards, fliers, and an initial advertising budget. If you also have access to reliable transportation and really want to kick-start marketing efforts, offer customers free, fast, and convenient laundry pick up and delivery. Don't worry if you can't offer this service because customers can simply drop off their laundry and return at a later date to pick it up. Design fliers describing your laundry cleaning service and post these on community bulletin boards commonly found at fitness centers, grocery markets, and gas stations. Also run cheap classified ads, and most important, call on businesses, such as police and fire services, restaurants, grocers, fitness clubs, spas, and hair salons that use laundry services to land large-volume accounts. Most commercial laundries charge by the pound, so check around your area to see what the competition is charging. Remember, you can charge extra for services such as ironing, stain removal, zipper repair, alterations, and button replacements.

Washing Windows

There are a great number of benefits to starting a part-time window washing service, including proven demand, low start-up costs, no special skill requirements, flexible working hours, and the best news, great moneymaking potential. Combined, these benefits create a very persuasive argument for energetic young people to start their own window washing service working on weekends and during the summer holiday. You can market a window washing service by designing, printing, and hand delivering simple fliers describing your service to home and business owners. You can also run low-cost classified advertisements in your local community newspaper under the home services section, And, you can piggyback your service with existing businesses such as house painters, window installers, property managers, real estate agents, and renovation contractors, that commonly require window washers, or that can refer your service to their customers. Basic equipment such as ladders, buckets, and squeegees, as well as suitable transportation, will be needed, but all of these can be bought inexpensively. Offering clients compatible services such as rain gutter cleaning and pressure washing is a great way to increase profits. Companies like ABC Window Cleaning Supply ♂ www.window-cleaning-supply.com, sell window cleaning products and equipment.

Residential Cleaning

Residential house and apartment cleaners perform duties such as dusting, vacuuming, washing surfaces, mopping floors, polishing mirrors and fixtures, and some also offer interior window washing. Needless to say, the work is easy and requires no special skills, which means all young people are qualified to start a part-time residential house cleaning service. For the most part residential cleaners supply all cleaning supplies and equipment needed to perform these services. Therefore, you will need to invest in things such as a vacuum cleaner, buckets, dusters, mops, rags, cleaning solvents, a stepladder, and reliable transportation, or work close to home and use public transit. Ideally, you want to land customers who will be using the service on a regular basis not just occasionally. That way you will not constantly need to find new customers. Get started by first asking family, friends, and neighbors if they are looking for a part-time house cleaner. If this route does not pan out you can market your services with flier and coupon drops, as well as by running cheap classified advertisements in your local newspaper. If you get really busy, or want to expand the business, simply hire school friends to help out. On average, most cleaners charge in the vicinity of $15 per hour.

Office Cleaning

Like residential cleaning, commercial cleaning is a booming industry generating billions in sales. Commercial cleaners basically perform the same services as residential cleaners—dusting, vacuuming, and polishing, but on a larger scale and with the addition of services like replenishing paper products, soaps, washing windows, stripping floors, and emptying trash and recycling receptacles. The only downside to commercial cleaning is that in most cases the cleaning must be performed nights or weekends after the office closes, which is actually a positive for young people going to college. Rates generally tend to be higher for commercial cleaning as opposed to residential cleaning, in the range of $20 to $30 per hour, plus paper and other specialized supplies. This is because equipment costs are higher, work such as floor stripping and waxing is more specialized, and once again, the nighttime aspect of the work enables you to charge a premium. Landing office-cleaning work requires nothing more than getting out to knock on doors to pitch the benefits of your services—reliability, quality, and good value. A good book about starting a cleaning service is 📖 *Start Your Own Cleaning Service* by Jacquelyn Lynn (Entrepreneur Press, 2003). This book provides all the inside information and tips you need to know to get started making money right away.

Construction Site Clean-Up

Operating a construction clean-up service is a bit different than a residential or office cleaning service mainly because there is often heavy lifting, ladder work, and some debris removal required. Therefore, this opportunity is best suited for fit young adults with access to reliable transportation. Construction clean-up crews are the people that make sure newly built or renovated homes are spic and span before the owners move in and take possession. Duties generally include cleaning windows inside and outside, dusting and washing all surfaces, removing stickers on windows and appliances, hauling away the last of the construction debris, picking up dropped nails, polishing all the interior glass, marble, and tile surfaces, dusting and washing walls and ceilings, and vacuuming the floors. As a rule of thumb, you provide the contractor or homeowner with an estimate prior to doing the work, and rates vary greatly depending on the size of the job and scope of the work, but expect to earn in the $30 an hour range. Because the work is more involved, it might be a good idea to have a number of friends on standby to work as needed. Renovation companies, contractors, and property developers are all potential customers. And one of the best ways to land new business is to simply create a promotional flier describing your construction clean-up services and hand deliver this to these types of potential customers in your local area. Once you are established, you will generally find that repeat and referral business will keep you busy and earning an excellent income working nights and weekends.

Graffiti Removal

Graffiti is everywhere you look, on walls, sidewalks, signs, and fences, which makes starting a graffiti removal service an excellent choice for young entrepreneurs. Removing graffiti does not require a great deal of experience; it can be learned on the job with practice. The equipment required is a portable pressure washer and suitable transportation. But to keep start-up costs low you can rent a power washer as needed and purchase one later from the profits you earn removing graffiti. Graffiti Genies, located online at ♂ www.graffitigenies.com, sells graffiti removal equipment and supplies, and they even provide graffiti removal training. Once you're up and running one marketing option is to visit businesses that are often the victims of graffiti vandalism and offer them a low-cost graffiti removal solution. Provide clients with a monthly graffiti removal option which for a fixed monthly fee, you will check in once a week to see if there is any new graffiti to be removed. If new graffiti is present, you simply remove it. If no graffiti is present, you move on to the next customer. In addition to business owners, graffiti removal services can also be marketed to schools, libraries, homeowners, and just about any other location with graffiti problems.

Clean Rain Gutters

Armed with nothing more than a ladder, garden hose, rope, a safety harness, and basic transportation, it is possible to earn as much as $200 to $300 per day on weekends cleaning leaves and other debris from rain gutters. Safety is the first concern when cleaning rain gutters because you will be working off a ladder and on the roof and often as high as 20 feet in the air. Therefore, you need to take all safety precautions before getting started and feel comfortable working at heights. You can market your gutter cleaning services by designing a simple flier outlining the details of your service along with contact information. Hand deliver the fliers to homes throughout your neighborhood; be sure to advertise a special promotion on the flier to help secure work quickly such as a 20 percent discount. You can also take the fliers to bulletin boards in the community, and talk with roofing and painting contractors so that they can refer your service to their customers. Ideally, you want all customers to become repeat customers. Because rain gutters need to be cleaned in the fall and spring, it is a good idea to get customers to sign up for yearly gutter cleaning.

Awning Cleaning

If you are searching for the perfect part-time moneymaking gig, then you might be interested in knowing that cleaning awnings requires no previous experience and you can earn upwards of $30 per hour. Many businesses have, and continue to switch from traditional box signs to commercial awning signs and all of these awnings have one thing in common: they need to be cleaned on a regular basis. A dirty awning does not project a good corporate image. This in turn creates a great opportunity for the enterprising young entrepreneur to cash in and profit by start-ing an awning cleaning service. The best way to get customers is simply to put on a pair of comfortable walking shoes and start knocking on doors. Visit retailers and offices in your area that have awning signs and pitch your service. This may seem like an old-fashioned way to promote the service, but just think, if you talk with five potential customers a day and can close one, you will have ten repeat customers in a couple of weeks' time. You will need basic equipment such as a lad-der, buckets, a hose, and scrub brushes, but this kind of equipment is cheap to purchase. Awning Cleaning Source found online at ♂ www.awningcleaning source.com, sells awning cleaning equipment and supplies.

Carpet and Upholstery Cleaning

What makes starting and operating a carpet and upholstery service such a great new business venture for young entrepreneurs? There are lots of reasons, such as low investment, minimal skill requirements, part-time hours, and proven demand. If these are not enough reasons to tempt you to start a carpet cleaning service, per-haps the fact that you can earn upwards of $30 per hour will! So what will you need to get started? Not much. In addition to reliable transportation, you will need to purchase carpet and upholstery cleaning equipment and supplies, which can be bought online from sellers such as Advantage Cleaning Systems, ♂ www.start cleaning.com, or Rotovac, ♂ www.carpet-cleaning-equipment.com. If your investment budget is tight, consider renting a carpet-cleaning machine for each job and purchase one down the road from the profits you make. Carpet and upholstery cleaning is relatively easy, and can be mastered with a little practice. Cleaning carpets at home and for neighbors is a great way to learn what you need to know before you start charging for your services. A fast-start method for secur-ing work is to print and distribute two-for-one coupons. "Have one room of car-pet cleaned and get a second room of carpet cleaned for free." Or, "Let us clean your couch and we'll steam clean your loveseat for free." You will also want to focus much of your marketing efforts on securing customers that will become reg-ulars, or refer their clients to your business. This will include property managers, real estate agents, landlords, retailers, car dealers, used furniture stores, and RV dealers.

Clean Washrooms

Bad food and dirty washrooms are the two most common reasons why people will not return to a restaurant. This fact alone can be used as your number one sales and marketing tool for convincing restaurant owners and managers that they need your washroom sanitizing services. Concentrate your marketing efforts on busy fast food restaurants, family restaurants, coffee shops, and donut shops, and others with high customer turnover—businesses that stand to benefit the most in terms of customer satisfaction from a daily washroom sanitizing service. Outside of reliable transportation, basic cleaning equipment and supplies, and a strong work ethic, other requirements to start this service add up to nothing more than a cell phone and business cards. Call on restaurant owners and managers directly to pitch the benefits of your service in person, and remember to stay close to the core sales argument—people seldom return to a restaurant if the washrooms are dirty. Charging $6 to $12 per washroom may not seem like a lot of money, but considering the average washroom will only take 10 to 20 minutes to fully clean and sanitize, you stand to earn upwards of $50 an hour during nights and weekends even allowing for travel time between jobs.

Clean Blinds

Wood, plastic, or fabric window blinds are the most popular window covering choice for homes and offices in North America. So with millions of window blinds needing to be cleaned regularly, it makes a lot of sense to cash in by starting a blind cleaning service. The most efficient way to clean window blinds is by using ultrasonic cleaning equipment, which is basically a tank filled with cleaning solution that gently cleans blinds ultrasonically with no risk of damaging the blind's structural materials or operational parts. This equipment can be mounted in a van or trailer so you can offer blind cleaning services onsite, or you can set up the cleaning equipment at home or in a warehouse space and offer clients free pickup, delivery, and reinstallation after the blinds have been cleaned. There are a number of companies selling blind cleaning equipment, such as Hang & Shine, ♂ www.dirty blinds.com, and S. Morantz Inc., ♂ www.morantz.com. Of course, if funds are tight, you can always clean blinds by hand using dusters and rags. In addition to homeowners, also be sure to aim your marketing efforts toward capturing blind cleaning contracts for schools, hospitals, hotels, institutions, corporations, and others with large numbers of window blinds. This is a great weekend business that really has the potential to generate big profits.

17

ENTERTAINMENT-RELATED BUSINESSES

Calling all aspiring stars! Starting an entertainment-related business might just be right up your alley, not to mention also potentially very profitable. There are numerous ways to earn a ton of extra cash in the entertainment industry, and have a whole lot of fun doing it. You can launch an acting or modeling career, spin records for big profits by becoming a weekend disc jockey, operate an entertainment booking service, or even plan and host events for young people. The choices are nearly unlimited.

Organize Children's Parties

What are the two most important prerequisites for starting and operating a children's party service? I'm glad you asked. They are a love of children and a love for party planning. Just think of all of the reasons a party is thrown for kids—birthdays, milestones, school-is-out, back-to-school, holidays like Easter and Valentine's, special achievements in sports and academics, and recovery from illness. As the official party planner your duties are to plan the party, decorate with balloons, streamers, and party favors, provide entertainment like clowns, music, and magicians, serve lots of food, beverages, and desserts, stage fun games and contests giving away lots of neat prizes, and make the event one heck of a lot of fun for kids and their parents. The rates you can charge will vary depending on the menu, entertainments, games, and frills, but you can start at about $20 per guest and go as high as $100 per guest for highly specialized and themed parties. There are good books about how to organize and host parties for kids such as ▢ *The Ultimate Birthday Party Book: 50 Complete and Creative Themes to Make Your Kid's Special Day Fantastic* by Susan Batters (Chariot Victor Publishing, 2002).

Be a Star

The motion picture and television film production industry is booming, and you can cash in and secure your 15 minutes of fame by becoming an actor or a film extra, otherwise known as a background performer. What makes working in film such a great opportunity for kids, teens, and young adults is that people of every type are needed to fill acting rolls and as background performers, which is especially true of extra work because you do not need any specialized actors' training or previous acting experience. Motion pictures, television shows, commercials, and music videos are filmed just about anywhere, but the big film production centers in North America are Los Angeles, Vancouver, New York, Toronto, Miami, and Montreal. Becoming a film extra is simple. Get started by visiting the web site of the Screen Actors Guild (SAG), ♂ www.sag.org in the United States, or the Alliance of Canadian Cinema Television and Radio Artist (ACTRA), ♂ www .actra.ca, in Canada to get a list of "extras casting services and agents." The next step is to contact one of these services and sign up as a client. That's about it. When they have work for you they will call and give you the details, such as casting call time and location, as well as special requests such as wardrobe needs. You will start out as a nonunion extra until you qualify to be a member of the SAG in the United States, and ACTRA in Canada. The difference between the two is nonunion performers earn substantially less than union performers. Rates for extra work start about $10 an hour, with a minimum of eight hours' pay guaranteed, but can range as high as $20 an hour for specialty extra and stand-in jobs.

Spin Records

If you love music and love to have fun, then starting a disc jockey service might be the perfect way for you to earn a ton of extra cash. Disc jockey services are always in high demand. Even better, rates are in the range of $250 to $500 per event, plus tips! Just think, a mere 20 disc jockey gigs a year can earn up to an extra $10,000. So now that you have heard the good news, here is the other side of the coin: You will need to invest some money buying equipment, music, setting up your business, and to cover initial advertising. In total expect to invest in the range of $10,000, although you can do it for less by purchasing used equipment in good condition. You will also need an excellent and varied music selection, reliable transportation, as well as an outgoing personality and talent for public speaking. Potential clients include event and wedding planners, tour operators, restaurants, corporations, teen raves, and people hosting private parties and functions. Lots of helpful information about starting a disc jockey service can be obtained in the United States from the American Disc Jockey Association, ☎ (888) 723-5776, ✆ www.adja.org, or in Canada from the Canadian Disc Jockey Association, ☎ (877) 472-0653, ✆ www.cdja.org.

Party-in-a-Box

Starting a party-in-a-box business is a great way for teens and young adults to earn a ton of extra cash. With everybody leading such busy lives, who has time to stop and buy all of the paper products and novelty items needed to throw one heck of a party? Few people, and that is what makes this business a red-hot money-making opportunity. The premise of the business is very straightforward. Simply, prepare all of the products people need to throw a party, all conveniently packaged in one box. Your customers simply open the box, decorate the party location, hand out the party favors to guests, and that's it. Depending on the theme of the party—children's birthday, adult birthday, retirement, anniversary, special achievement, engagement, wedding, Christmas, News Year's, Fourth of July, and more—each box can contain hats, flowers, banners, ribbons, balloons, pi–atas, invitations, streamers, glow sticks, noisemakers, games, confetti, and other party supplies specific to the event. All of these products can be purchase at deeply discounted wholesale prices from any number of party product distributors, such as American Party Company, ✆ www.epartysite.com, and the Party and Paper

Warehouse, ✆ www.partyandpaperwarehouse.com, or from a party product wholesaler in your local area. Advertise in your local newspaper and pin promotional fliers to bulletin boards; also be sure to call event and party planners, restaurants, and day-care centers to let them know about your business because all can become a good source for new and referral business.

Party Balloons

An investment of less than $1,000 can get you started in your own part-time party balloon business, and on your way to earning big profits on weekends and during holidays. Corporate events, grand openings, children's birthday parties, special occasions, graduations, retailer sales, weddings, and community events, concerts, and parades: The demand for party balloons is gigantic and ever growing. Marketing a party balloon service is easy; simply design a basic, yet detailed promotional flier describing your service and rates. Deliver the flier to party and event planners, wedding planners, children stores, restaurants, banquet facilities, day-care centers, and catering companies in your local area. Because balloon decoration services are in high demand it won't take long for your telephone to start ringing with customers lining up to hire your service. You will need reliable transportation and basic equipment such as helium tanks for gas-filled balloons and air compressors for blowing up cold-air balloons, but don't worry, this type of equipment is cheap to buy or rent. You can purchase wholesale balloons and related equipment online through businesses such as Balloons Online, ✆ www.balloons.com, B&C Balloons, ✆ www.bcballons.net, and Wholesale Balloons, ✆ www.wholesale balloons.com.

Entertainment Booking Service

Kids parties, corporate events, social events, graduations, birthdays, anniversaries, weddings, trade shows, conventions, and Christmas parties are a lot more fun when there is live entertainment to keep guests entertained and in high spirits. That is why there is big part-time money to be earned by operating your own party entertainment booking service providing live entertainment for parties and special occasions. Entertainers can include clowns, soloists, musical bands, magicians, singing telegrams, public speakers, spokespeople, acrobats, jugglers, and comedians. You can employ these kinds of entertainers on a contract working on an on-call basis, and charge them either a fee for listing with your service or a revenue share split every time they work. Promote the service by running advertisements in your local newspaper and by contacting wedding planners and event planners in your community and explaining the various types of entertainers your service provides, as well as your rates. This service can easily be managed from home or your dorm room. Start-up costs are modest with the bulk of the budget being spent on marketing to get the telephone ringing with eager customers wanting to book acts for their next special occasion or event.

Rent Bounce Houses

That's right, you can bounce your way to big profits by starting a bouncy house rental business. Bouncy houses are inflatable amusement games that children and adults absolutely love to bounce around in and on. They are available in a wide range of shapes, sizes, and themes such as castles and hot air blimps. Renting bouncy houses is easy and you can make incredible profits, up to $250 per day, just for delivering, setting up, and breaking them down after the event, making this one of the best part-time business opportunities available for young entrepreneurs. New inflatable amusement games costs in the range of $2,000 for small basic models, and up to $15,000 for large fully-featured models. The investment is high, but the return on investment is excellent. If your budget is tight, you can purchase used inflatables for about half the cost of new. Bouncy house inflatables can be rented for children's birthday parties, to charities for community events, sports and social clubs, and for corporate events. Set up is fast, and can be done by one person in approximately 30 minutes; plan about the same amount of time for dismantling and removal. There are many companies manufacturing and selling inflatable amusement products, such as China Inflatable, ♂ www.china-inflatable.com, Discount Inflatable, ♂ www.discountinflatable.com, and Moon Walker, ♂ www.moon-walker.com.

Romantic Catering Service

Who needs cupid when they can hire your romantic catering service and surprise that someone special in their lives with a unique and unforgettable romantic dinner for two? You plan and play host to a memorable dining experience for clients. Your service would provide the gourmet meal, make all the arrangements, supply the transportation, and even serve the meal on the finest china while dressed in exquisite formal wear. Best of all, you do not need to be a chef, have the horse-drawn carriage, or even have the ability to serve the meal. All of these can be contracted to qualified people with the skills and equipment. What is required, however, is the ability to market the service and have the creative imagination to plan the best romantic dinner adventure possible. Just think, the evening could start with a ride in a horse-drawn carriage through the park and end on a secluded beach under the stars where clients would dine on lobster and caviar picnic-style.

Karaoke Host

A terrific opportunity exists for young people that "have the pipes" and the outgoing personality to start a karaoke host service. Karaoke is wildly popular and to back this up you do not have to look any further than your own community, as I am sure there are lots of karaoke singing nights. The requirements for starting a karaoke host service are very basic: You need karaoke equipment and a varied music selection, and of course, the ability to sing, or at the least not send people running from the building with their ears covered. You can market your service to event and wedding planners as well as to local restaurants and pubs that might like to hold a weekly karaoke singing contest. Rates are currently in the range of $150 to $250 per event, plus gratuities. This is a venture that thrives on repeat business and word-of-mouth referrals. Therefore, smile and make sure that everyone has one heck of a good time. DTS Karaoke Wholesale, ♪ www.dtskaraoke.com, Karaoke Now, ♪ www .karaokenow.com, Karaoke Wholesale, ♪ www.karaoke-wholesale.com, all sell karaoke equipment and music at discount wholesale prices.

APPENDIX

A

BUSINESS ASSOCIATION RESOURCES

U.S. Business Associations

American Accounting Association
5717 Bessie Dr.
Sarasota, FL 34233
☎ (941) 921-7747
♂ www.aaahq.org/index.cfm

American Advertising Federation
1101 Vermont Ave. NW, #500
Washington, DC 20005
☎ (202) 898-0089
♂ www.aaf.org

American Association of Franchisees and Dealers
P.O. Box 81887
San Diego, CA 92138-1887

☎ (800) 733-9858
♂ www.aafd.org

American Bankers Association
1120 Connecticut Ave. NW
Washington, DC 20037
♂ www.aba.com

American Home Business Association
4505 S. Wasatch Blvd., #140
Salt Lake City, UT 84124
☎ (800) 664-2422,
♂ www.homebusiness.com

American Institute of Certified Public Accountants
1211 Ave. of the Americas

New York, NY 10036
☎ (212) 596-6200
♂ www.aicpa.org

American Marketing Association
311 S. Wacker Dr., #5800
Chicago, IL 60606
☎ (312) 542-9000
♂ www.ama.org

America's Community Bankers
900 19th St. NW, #400
Washington, DC 20006
☎ (202) 857-3100
♂ www.acbankers.org

Association of Credit and
Collection Professionals
P.O. Box 390106
Minneapolis, MN 55439
☎ (952) 926-6547
♂ www.ica-credit.org

Association of National Advertisers
708 Third Ave.
New York, NY 10017-4270
☎ (212) 697-5950
♂ www.ana.net

Association of Small Business
Development Centers
8990 Burke Lake Rd.
Burke, VA 22015
☎ (703) 764-9850
♂ www.asbdc-us.org

Commercial Finance Association
225 W. 34th St.
New York, NY 10122
☎ (212) 594-3490
♂ www.cfa.com

Direct Marketing Association
1120 Avenue of the Americas
New York, NY 10036
☎ (212) 768-7277
♂ www.the-dma.org

Equipment Leasing Association
of America
4301 N. Fairfax Dr., #550
Arlington, VA 22203
☎ (703) 527-8655
♂ www.elaonline.com

Independent Bankers Association of
America
1 Thomas Cir. NW, #400
Washington, DC 20005
☎ (202) 659-8111
♂ www.ibaa.org

Independent Insurance Agents of
America
127 S. Payton St.
Alexandria, VA 22314
☎ (800) 221-7917
♂ www.independentagent.com

Institute of Certified Management
Accountants
10 Paragon Dr.
Montvale, NJ 07645
☎ (800) 638-4427
♂ www.imanet.org

Marketing Research Association
1344 Silas Deane Hwy., #306
P.O. Box 230
Rocky Hill, CT 06067-0230
☎ (860) 257-4008
♂ www.mra-net.org

Mother's Home Business
Network
P.O. Box 423
East Meadow, NY 11554
☎ (516) 997-7394
🖫 www.homeworkingmom.com

The National Association for
the Self-Employed
P.O. Box 612067
DFW Airport
Dallas, TX 75261-2067
☎ (800) 232-6273
🖫 www.naseweb.org

National Association of Home
Based Businesses
10451 Mill Run Cir.
Owings Mills, MD 21117
☎ (410) 363-3698
🖫 www.usahomebusiness.com

National Business Incubation
Association
20 E. Circle Dr., #190
Athens, OH 45701-3751
☎ (740) 593-4331
🖫 www.nbia.org

National Inventors Foundation
403 S. Central Ave.
Glendale, CA 91204
☎ (818) 246-6546
🖫 www.inventions.org

National Venture Capital Association
1655 N. Ft. Myer Dr., #850
Arlington, VA 22209
☎ (703) 524-2549
🖫 www.nvca.org

Outdoor Advertising Association
of America
1850 M St. NW, #1040
Washington, DC 20036
☎ (202) 833-5566
🖫 www.oaaa.org

Radio Advertising Bureau
1320 Greenway Dr., #500
Irving, TX 75038
☎ (800) 232-3131
🖫 www.rab.com

Service Corps of Retired Executives
409 Third St. SW, 6th Fl.
Washington, DC 20024
☎ (800) 634-0245
🖫 www.score.org

Canadian Business Associations

Association of Canadian Advertisers
307-175 Bloor Street East, South Tower
Toronto, Ontario
Canada M4W 3R8
☎ (416) 964-3805
🖫 www.aca-online.com

Canadian Association of
Business Incubators
537-1071 King Street West
Toronto, Ontario
Canada M6K 3K2
☎ (416) 345-9937
🖫 www.cabi.ca

Canadian Association of
Family Enterprise
1388 C Cornwall Rd.

Oakville, Ontario
Canada L6J 7W5
☎ (866)-849-0099
♂ www.cafemembers.org

Canadian Bankers Association
P.O. Box 348
Commerce Court Postal Station
Toronto, Ontario
Canada M5L 1G2
☎ (800) 263-0231
♂ www.cba.ca

Canadian Bar Association
500-865 Carling Avenue
Ottawa, Ontario
Canada K1S 5S8
☎ (800) 267-8860
♂ www.cba.org

The Canadian Chamber of Commerce
BCE Place
181 Bay Street
Toronto, Ontario
Canada M5J 2T3
☎ (416) 868-6415
♂ www.chamber.ca

Canadian Council of Better Business Bureaus
800 2 St. Clair Avenue East
Toronto, Ontario
Canada M4T 2T5
☎ (416) 644-4936
♂ www.canadiancouncilbbb.ca

Canadian Finance and Leasing Association
301–15 Toronto Street
Toronto, Ontario
Canada M5C 2E3

☎ (416) 860-1133
♂ www.cfla-acfl.ca

The Canadian Institute of Chartered Accountants
277 Wellington Street West
Toronto, Ontario
Canada M5V 3H2
☎ (416) 977-3222
♂ www.cica.ca

Canadian Marketing Association
607–1 Concorde Gate
Don Mills, Ontario
Canada M3C 3N6
☎ (416) 391-2362
♂ www.the-cma.org

Canadian Newspaper Association
200–890 Yonge Street
Toronto, Ontario
Canada M4W 3P4
☎ (416) 923-3567
♂ www.cna-acj.ca

Canadian Public Relation Society
346–4195 Dundas Street West
Toronto, Ontario
Canada M8X 1Y4
☎ (416) 239-7034
♂ www.cprs.ca

Canadian Venture Capital Association
200–234 Eglington Avenue East
Toronto, Ontario
Canada M4P 1K5
☎ (416) 487-0519
♂ www.cvca.ca

Canadian Youth Business Foundation
1410–100 Adelaide Street West

Toronto, Ontario
Canada M5H 1S3
☎ (800) 464-2923
♂ www.cybf.ca

Certified General Accountants of Canada Association
800–1188 West Georgia Street
Vancouver, British Columbia
Canada V6E 4A2
☎ (604) 669-3555
♂ www.cga-online.org/canada

Certified Management Accountants of Canada
Mississauga Executive Centre
One Robert Speck Parkway, Suite 1400
Mississauga, Ontario
Canada L4Z 3M3
☎ (905) 949-4200
♂ www.cma-canada.org

Commercial Finance Association
1500–141 Adelaide Street West
Toronto, Ontario
Canada M5H 3L5
☎ (416) 507-2673.
♂ www.cfa.com/Chapters/
chapters_list.htm

Insurance Brokers Association of Canada
1920–155 University Avenue
Toronto, Ontario
Canada M5H 3B7
☎ (416) 367-1831
♂ www.ibac.ca

International Internet Marketing Association
PO Box 4018

349 W. Georgia Street
Vancouver, British Columbia
Canada V6B 3Z4
♂ www.iimaonline.org

Marketing Research and Intelligence Association
310–2175 Sheppard Ave. East
North York, Ontario
Canada M2J 1W8
☎ (416) 493-4080
♂ www.mria-arim.ca

The Promotional Products Association of Canada
305–4920 de Maisonneuve West
Westmount, Québec
Canada H3Z 1N1
☎ (514) 489-5359
♂ www.promocan.com

Radio Marketing Bureau
316–175 Bloor Street East, North Tower
Toronto, Ontario
Canada M4W 3R8
☎ (416) 922-5757
♂ www.rmb.ca

Retail Council of Canada
800–1255 Bay Street
Toronto, Ontario
Canada M5R 2A9
☎ (416) 922-6678
♂ www.retailcouncil.org

SOHO Canada
324–1641 Lonsdale Avenue
North Vancouver, British Columbia
Canada V7M 2J5
☎ (604) 929-8250
♂ www.soho.ca

Television Bureau of Canada
1005-160 Bloor Street East
Toronto, Ontario
Canada M4W 1B9
☎ (416) 923-8813
♂ www.tvb.ca

***Young Entrepreneurs Association
(YEA)***
300-720 Spadina Avenue
Toronto, Ontario
Canada M5S 2T9
☎ (888) 639-3222
♂ www.yea.ca

U.S. GOVERNMENT RESOURCES

Government Agencies

Copyright Office
Library of Congress
101 Independence Ave. SE
Washington, DC 20559-6000
☎ (202) 707-3000
♪ www.loc.gov/copyright

Department of Agriculture
1400 Independence Ave. SW
Washington, DC 20250
☎ (202) 720-7420
♪ www.usda.gov

Department of Commerce
1401 Constitution Ave. NW

Washington, DC 20230
☎ (202) 482-2000
♪ www.doc.gov

Department of Labor
200 Constitution Ave. NW, Rm. S-1004
Washington, DC 20210
☎ (866) 487-2365
♪ www.dol.gov

Department of Treasury
Main Treasury Bldg.
1500 Pennsylvania Ave. NW
Washington, DC 20220
☎ (202) 622-2000
♪ www.ustreas.gov

Export-Import Bank of the United States
11 Vermont Ave. NW, #911
Washington, DC 20571
☎ (202) 565-3940
♂ www.exim.gov

Federal Communications Commission
445 12th St. SW
Washington, DC 20544
☎ (888) 225-5322
♂ www.fcc.gov

Federal Trade Commission
600 Pennsylvania Ave. NW
Washington, DC, 20580
☎ (202) 326-2222
♂ www.ftc.gov

Internal Revenue Service
1111 Constitution Ave. NW
Washington, DC 20224
☎ (202) 622-5000
♂ www.irs.ustreas.gov

U.S. Food and Drug Administration
5600 Fishers Lane
Rockville, MD 20857
☎ (888) 463-6332
♂ www.fda.gov

U.S. Patent and Trademark Office
Crystal Plaza 3, Rm. 2C02
Washington, DC 20231
☎ (800) 786-9199
♂ www.uspto.gov

Small Business Administration (SBA)
409 Third St. SW
Washington, DC 20416
☎ (800) 827-5722
♂ www.sba.gov

Small Business Administration (SBA) District Offices

The SBA has several types of field offices. The district offices offer the fullest range of services. To access all district office web sites, go to ♂ www.sba.gov/regions/states.html.

Alabama
801 Tom Martin Drive
Birmingham, AL 35211
☎ (205) 290-7101

Alaska
510 L St., #310
Anchorage, AK 99501
☎ (907) 271-4022

Arizona
2828 N. Central Ave., #800
Phoenix, AZ 85004-1093
☎ (602) 745-7200

Arkansas
2120 Riverfront Dr., #100
Little Rock, AR 72202
☎ (501) 324-5871

California
2719 Air Fresno Dr., #200
Fresno, CA 93727-1547
☎ (559) 487-5791

330 N. Brand Blvd., #1200
Glendale, CA 91203-2304
☎ (818) 552-3210

550 W. C St., #550
San Diego, CA 92101
☎ (619) 557-7250

455 Market St., 6th Fl.

San Francisco, CA 94105-1988
☎ (415) 744-6820

650 Capitol Mall, #7-500
Sacramento, CA 95814-2413
☎ (916) 930-3700

200 W. Santa Ana Blvd., #700
Santa Ana, CA 92701-4134
☎ (714) 550-7420

Colorado
721 19th St., #426
Denver, CO 80202-2517
☎ (303) 844-2607

Connecticut
330 Main St., 2nd Fl.
Hartford, CT 06106-1800
☎ (860) 240-4700

Delaware
824 N. Market St., #610
Wilmington, DE 19801-3011
☎ (302) 573-6294

District of Columbia
1110 Vermont Ave. NW, #900
Washington, DC 20005
☎ (202) 606-4000

Florida
100 S. Biscayne Blvd., 7th Floor
Miami, FL 33131-2011
☎ (305) 536-5521

7825 Baymeadows Way, #100-B
Jacksonville, FL 32256-7504
☎ (904) 443-1900

Georgia
233 Peachtree St. NE, #1900
Atlanta, GA 30303
☎ (404) 331-0100

Hawaii
300 Ala Moana Blvd., Room 2-235
Box 50207
Honolulu, III 96850-4981
☎ (808) 541-2990

Idaho
1020 Main St., #290
Boise, ID 83702-5745
☎ (208) 334-1696

Illinois
500 W. Madison St., #1250
Chicago, IL 60661-2511
☎ (312) 353-4528

511 W. Capitol Ave., #302
Springfield, IL 62704
☎ (217) 492-4416

Indiana
429 N. Pennsylvania St., #100
Indianapolis, IN 46204-1873
☎ (317) 226-7272

Iowa
Mail Code 0736
The Lattner Bldg.
215 Fourth Ave. SE, #200
Cedar Rapids, IA 52401-1806
☎ (319) 362-6405

210 Walnut St., Rm. 749
Des Moines, IA 50309-2186
☎ (515) 284-4422

Kansas
271 W. Third St. N., #2500
Wichita, KS 67202-1212
☎ (316) 269-6616

Kentucky
600 Dr. Martin Luther King Jr. Pl., #188

Louisville, KY 40202
☎ (502) 582-5761

Louisiana
365 Canal St., #2820
New Orleans, LA 70130
☎ (504) 589-6685

Maine
Edward S. Muskie Federal Bldg.
68 Sewall St., Rm. 512
Augusta, ME 04330
☎ (207) 622-8274

Maryland
10 S. Howard St., #6220
Baltimore, MD 21201-2525
☎ (410) 962-4392

Massachusetts
10 Causeway St., Rm. 265
Boston, MA 02222-1093
☎ (617) 565-5590

Michigan
McNamara Bldg.
477 Michigan Ave., Rm. 515
Detroit, MI 48226
☎ (313) 226-6075

Minnesota
Butler Square 210-C
100 N. Sixth St.
Minneapolis, MN 55403
☎ (612) 370-2324

Mississippi
AmSouth Bank Plaza
210 E. Capitol St., #900
Jackson, MS 39201
☎ (601) 965-4378

Missouri
323 W. Eighth St., #501
Kansas City, MO 64105
☎ (816) 374-6708

815 Olive St., Rm. 242
St. Louis, MO 63101
☎ (314) 539-6600

Montana
Federal Building,
10 W. 15th St., #1100
Helena, MT 59626
☎ (800) 776-9144

Nebraska
11145 Mill Valley Rd.
Omaha, NE 68154
☎ (402) 221-4691

Nevada
300 S. Las Vegas Blvd., #1100
Las Vegas, NV 89101
☎ (702) 388-6611

New Hampshire
143 N. Main St., #202
Concord, NH 03301-1248
☎ (603) 225-1400

New Jersey
2 Gateway Center, 15th Fl.
Newark, NJ 07102
☎ (973) 645-2434

New Mexico
625 Silver Ave. SW, #320
Albuquerque, NM 87102
☎ (505) 346-7909

New York
111 W. Huron St., #1311

Buffalo, NY 14202
☎ (716) 551-4301

26 Federal Plaza, #3100
New York, NY 10278
☎ (212) 264-4354

401 S. Salina St., 5th Fl.
Syracuse, NY 13202-2415
☎ (315) 471-9393

North Carolina
6302 Fairview Rd., #300
Charlotte, NC 28210-2227
☎ (704) 344-6563

North Dakota
657 Second Ave. N., Rm. 219
Fargo, ND 58108
☎ (701) 239-5131

Ohio
1111 Superior Ave., #630
Cleveland, OH 44114-2507
☎ (216) 522-4180

2 Nationwide Plaza, #1400
Columbus, OH 43215-2542
☎ (614) 469-6860

Oklahoma
210 Park Ave., #1300
Oklahoma City, OK 73102
☎ (405) 231-5521

Oregon
1515 SW Fifth Ave., #1050
Portland, OR 97201-5494
☎ (503) 326-2682

Pennsylvania
Robert N.C.

Nix Federal Bldg.
900 Market St., 5th Fl.
Philadelphia, PA 19107
☎ (215) 580-2722

Federal Bldg., Rm. 1128
1000 Liberty Ave.
Pittsburgh, PA 15222-4004
☎ (412) 395-6560

Puerto Rico
Citibank Tower
252 Ponce de Leon Blvd., #201
Hato Rey, PR 00918
☎ (787) 766-5572

Rhode Island
380 Westminster St., 5th Fl.
Providence, RI 02903
☎ (401) 528-4561

South Carolina
1835 Assembly St., Rm. 358
Columbia, SC 29201
☎ (803) 765-5377

South Dakota
110 S. Phillips Ave., #200
Sioux Falls, SD 57102-1109
☎ (605) 330-4231

Tennessee
50 Vantage Wy., #201
Nashville, TN 37228-1500
☎ (615) 736-5881

Texas
4300 Amon Carter Blvd., #114
Ft. Worth, TX 75155
☎ (817) 885-5500

8701 S. Gessner Dr., #1200
Houston, TX 77074
☎ (713) 773-6500

222 E. Van Buren St., Rm. 500
Harlingen, TX 78550-6855
☎ (956) 427-8533

1205 Texas Ave., Rm. 408
Lubbock, TX 79401-2693
☎ (806) 472-7462

Federal Bldg., 5th Fl.
727 E. Durango Blvd., Rm. A-527
San Antonio, TX 78206-1204
☎ (210) 472-5900

Utah
125 S. State St., Rm. 2231
Salt Lake City, UT 84138-1195
☎ (801) 524-3209

Vermont
87 State St., Rm. 205
Box 605
Montpelier, VT 05601
☎ (802) 828-4422

Virginia
Federal Bldg.
400 N. Eighth St., #1150
Richmond, VA 23240
☎ (804) 771-2400

Washington
1200 Sixth Ave., #1700
Seattle, WA 98101-1128
☎ (206) 553-7310

Spokane Regional Business Center
801 W. Riverside Ave., #200
Spokane, WA 99201
☎ (509) 353-2800

West Virginia
320 W. Pike St., #330
Clarksburg, WV 26301
☎ (304) 623-5631

Wisconsin
740 Regent St., #100
Madison, WI 53715
☎ (608) 441-5263

Wyoming
100 E. B St., Rm. 4001
P.O Box 2839
Casper, WY 82602-2839
☎ (307) 261-6500

Small Business Development Centers (SBDCs)

The following SBDCs can direct you to the SBDC in your region. You can access all SBDC web sites at ♂ www .sba.gov/sbdc and then click on "Your Nearest SBDC."

Alabama
University of Alabama
Box 870223
Tuscaloosa, AL 35487
☎ (205) 348-7443

Alaska
University of Alaska, Anchorage
430 W. Seventh Ave., #110
Anchorage, AK 99501
☎ (907) 274-7232

Arizona
2411 W. 14th St., #132
Tempe, AZ 85281
☎ (480) 731-8720

Arkansas
University of Arkansas, Little Rock
2801 S. University Ave.
Little Rock, AR 72204
☎ (501) 324-9043

California
San Joaquin Delta College
445 N. San Joaquin St.
Stockton, CA 95202
☎ (209) 943-5089

Colorado
Colorado Business Assistance Center
2413 Washington St.
Denver, CO 80205
☎ (303) 592-5920

Connecticut
University of Connecticut
2100 Hillside Rd., #1041
Storrs, CT 06269-1041
☎ (860) 486-4135

Delaware
University of Delaware
1 Innovation Wy., #301
Newark, DE 19711
☎ (302) 831-1555

District of Columbia
Howard University School of Business
2600 Sixth St. NW, Rm. 128
Washington, DC 20059
☎ (202) 806-1550

Florida
19 W. Garden St., #300
Pensacola, FL 32501
☎ (850) 470-4980

Georgia
University of Georgia

Chicopee Complex
1180 E. Broad St.
Athens, GA 30602-5412
☎ (706) 542-7436

Guam
Pacific Islands, UOG Station
Mangilao, Guam 96923
☎ (671) 735-2590

Hawaii
University of Hawaii, Hilo
200 W. Kawili St.
Hilo, HI 96720-4091
☎ (800) 897-4456

Idaho
Boise State University
1910 University Dr.
Boise, ID 83725-1655
☎ (208) 426-1640

Illinois
Greater North Pulaski
4054 W. North Ave.
Chicago, IL 60639
☎ (800) 252-2923

Indiana
1 N. Capitol Ave., #900
Indianapolis, IN 46204
☎ (317) 234-2082

Iowa
137 Lynn Ave., #5
Ames, IA 50014
☎ (515) 292-6351

Kansas
137 Skirk Hall
1501 S. Joplin St.
Pittsburg, KS 66762
☎ (620) 235-4920

Kentucky
600 Dr. MLK Jr. PL
Louisville, KY 40202
☎ (502) 582-5971

Louisiana
University of Louisiana at Monroe
Administration 2-57
Monroe, LA 71209-6435
☎ (318) 342-5506

Maine
University of Southern Maine
96 Falmouth St.
PO Box 9300
Portland, ME 04104-9300
☎ (207) 780-4420

Maryland
7100 E. Baltimore Ave., #402
College Park, MD 20740-3627
☎ (301) 403-8300

Massachusetts
University of Massachusetts
205 School of Management
PO Box 34935
Amherst, MA 01003
☎ (413) 545-6301

Michigan
Grand Valley State University
Seidman School of Business
510 W. Fulton St.
Grand Rapids, MI 49504
☎ (616) 336-7480

Minnesota
100 Metro Sq., 121 Seventh Pl.
St. Paul, MN 55101-2146
☎ (651) 296-5205

Mississippi
University of Mississippi
PO Box 1848
B 19 Jeanette Phillips Dr.
University, MS 38677-1848
☎ (662) 915-5001

Missouri
1205 University Pl., #1800
Columbia, MO 65211
☎ (573) 882-7096

Montana
1424 Ninth Ave.
Helena, MT 59620
☎ (406) 444-4780

Nebraska
College of Business Administration
60th and Dodge St., Rm. 407
Omaha, NE 68182-0248
☎ (402) 554-2521

Nevada
University of Nevada at Reno
CBA, MS 32
Reno, NV 89557-0100
☎ (702) 784-1717

New Hampshire
670 N. Commercial St., 4th Fl., #25
Manchester, NH 03101
☎ (603) 624-2000

New Jersey
49 Bleeker St.
Newark, NJ 07102-1913
☎ (973) 353-1927

New Mexico
Santa Fe Community College
Lead Center

6401 S. Richards Ave.
Santa Fe, NM 87508
☎ (800) 281-7232

New York
University at Albany
One Pinnacle Plaza, #218
Albany, NY 12203
☎ (518) 453-9567

North Carolina
SB & TDC
5 W. Hargett St., #600
Raleigh, NC 27601-1348
☎ (800) 258-0862

North Dakota
University of North Dakota
118 Gamble Hall
P.O Box 7308
Grand Forks, ND 58202
☎ (800) 445-7232

Ohio
37 N. High St.
Columbus, OH 43215
☎ (614) 221-1321

Oklahoma
Southeastern Oklahoma State University
517 W. University Blvd.
Durant, OK 74701
☎ (580) 745-7577

Oregon
44 W. Broadway, #501
Eugene, OR 97401-3021
☎ (541) 726-2250

Pennsylvania
University of Pennsylvania
Vance Hall

3733 Spruce St., 4th Fl.
Philadelphia, PA 19104
☎ (215) 898-1219

Rhode Island
Bryant College
1150 Douglas Pike
Smithfield, RI 02917
☎ (401) 232-6111

South Carolina
University of South Carolina
The Darla Moore School of Business
Columbia, SC 29208
☎ (803) 777-4907

South Dakota
University of South Dakota
School of Business
414 E. Clark St.
Vermillion, SD 57069-2390
☎ (605) 677-5011

Tennessee
University of Memphis
South Campus, Bldg. 1
Box 526324,
Memphis, TN 38152
☎ (901) 678-2500

Texas
2302 Fannin St., #200
Houston, TX 77002
☎ (713) 752-8444

Utah
125 S. State St., Rm. 2231
Salt Lake City, UT 84111
☎ (801) 957-3840

Vermont
PO Box 188

Randolph Center, VT 05061-0188
☎ (800) 464-7232

Virginia
116 E. Franklin St., #100
Richmond, VA 23219
☎ (804) 783-9314

Washington
Washington State University
PO Box 644851
Pullman, WA 99164-4851
☎ (509) 335-1576

West Virginia
State Capitol Complex
Bldg. 6, Rm. 652
1900 Kanawha Blvd. E.
Charleston, WV 25305
☎ (888) 982-7732

Wisconsin
University of Wisconsin
2000 Carlson Hall
Whitewater, WI 53190
☎ (800) 621-7235

Wyoming
111 W. Second St., #502
Casper, WY 82601
☎ (307) 234-6683

C

CANADIAN GOVERNMENT RESOURCES

Government Agencies

Government of Canada
Service Canada
Ottawa, Ontario
Canada K1A 0J9
☎ (800) 755-7047
♪ www.canada.gc.ca

Canada Revenue Agency
333 Laurier Avenue W.
Ottawa, Ontario
Canada K1A 0L9
☎ (800) 959-2221
♪ www.cra-arc.gc.ca

Canadian Intellectual Property Office (CIPO)
Patents, Trademarks, and Copyrights
Industry Canada, Place Du Portage
50 Victoria Street, 2nd Floor
Hull, Quebec
Canada K19 0C9
☎ (819) 997-1936
♪ www.cipo.gc.ca

Canadian Radio-Television and Telecommunications Commission (CRTC)
Ottawa, Ontario
Canada, K1A 0N2

☎ (877) 249-2782
♂ www.crtc.gc.ca

Canadian Tourism Commission
600–55 Metcalfe Street
Ottawa, Ontario
Canada K1P 6L5
♂ www.travelcanada.ca

Canadian Transportation Agency
Ottawa, Ontario
Canada K1A 0N9
☎ (888) 222-2592
♂ www.cta-otc.gc.ca

Export Development Canada
151 O'Connor
Ottawa, Ontario
Canada K1A 1K3
☎ (613) 598-2500
♂ www.edc.ca

Human Resources and Skills Development Canada
♂ www.hrsdc.gc.ca

International Trade Canada
125 Sussex Drive
Ottawa, Ontario
Canada K1A 0G2
☎ (613) 944-4000
♂ www.itcan-cican.gc.ca

National Research Council of Canada
NRC Corporate Communications
1200 Montreal Road, Bldg. M-58
Ottawa, Ontario
Canada K1A 0R6
☎ (613) 993-9101
♂ www.nrc-cnrc.gc.ca

Statistics Canada
120 Parkdale Avenue
Ottawa, Ontario
Canada K1A 0T6
☎ (800) 267-6677
♂ www.statcan.ca

Western Economic Diversification Canada
700–333 Seymour Street
Vancouver, British Columbia
Canada V6B 5G9
☎ (604) 666-6256
♂ www.wd.gc.ca

Canadian Business Service Centers (CBSCs)

Canadian Business Service Centers (CBSC), offer a wide range of products and services to assist entrepreneurs to start, grow, and manage their businesses. The federal government of Canada has partnered with provincial governments and private industry to develop Business Service Centers in all Canadian provinces and territories. CBSC products, services, and publications can be accessed on the CBSC web site at ♂ www.cbsc.org, or at any provincial CBSC location.

Alberta
100–10237–104th Street NW
Edmonton, Alberta
Canada T5J 1B1
☎ (800) 272-9675
♂ www.cbsc.org/alberta

British Columbia
601 West Cordova Street
Vancouver, British Columbia
Canada V6B 1G1
☎ (604) 775-5525
✆ www.smallbusinessbc.ca

Manitoba
250–240 Graham Avenue
Winnipeg, Manitoba
Canada R3C 4B3
☎ (800) 665-2019
✆ www.cbsc.org/manitoba

New Brunswick
570 Queen Street
Fredericton, New Brunswick
Canada E3B 6Z6
☎ (506) 444-6140
✆ www.cbsc.org/nb

Newfoundland and Labrador
90 O'Leary Avenue
St. John's, Newfoundland
Canada A3I 3T1
☎ (709) 772-6022
✆ www.cbsc.org/nf

Northwest Territories
PO Box 1320
Scotia Center, 8th Floor
Yellowknife, NT
Canada X1A 2L9
☎ (800) 661-0599
✆ www.cbsc.org/nwt

Nova Scotia
1575 Brunswick Street
Halifax, Nova Scotia
Canada B3J 2G1

☎ (902) 426-8604
✆ www.cbsc.org/ns

Nunavut
Parnaivik Building
PO Box 1000, Station 1198
Iqaluit, Nunavut
Canada X0A 0H0
☎ (877) 499-5199
✆ www.cbsc.org/nunavut

Ontario
North York Civic Center
500 Young Street
Toronto, Ontario
Canada M2N 5V7
☎ (800) 567-2345
✆ www.cbsc.org/ontario

Prince Edward Island
75 Fitzroy Street
Charlottetown, PEI
Canada C1A 7K2
☎ (902) 368-0771
✆ www.cbsc.org/pe

Quebec
5 Place Ville Marie
Suite 12500
Montreal, Quebec
Canada H3B 4Y2
☎ (800) 322-4636
✆ www.infoentrepreneurs.org

Saskatchewan
122 Third Avenue N
Saskatoon, Saskatchewan
Canada S7K 2H6
☎ (800) 667-4374
www.cbsc.org/sask

Yukon
101–307 Jarvis Street
Whitehorse, Yukon
Canada Y1A 2H3
☎ (800) 661-0543
www.cbsc.org/yukon

Business Development Bank of Canada (BDC)

Business Development Bank of Canada (BDC) is a financial institution owned by the government of Canada. BDC plays a leadership role in delivering financial, investment and consulting services to Canadian small businesses. Provincial BDC services are made available through a broad network of more than 80 branches stretching from coast to coast. To maximize the BDC reach, smaller and more remote communities are served through satellite branches, traveling account managers and consultants. Log onto provincial the main BDC web site to locate a branch office near you.

Business Development Bank of Canada
BDC Building
5 Place Ville Marie
Suite 400
Montréal, Québec
Canada H3B 5E7
☎ (877) 232-2269
♂ www.bdc.ca

Canadian Provincial Economic Development Offices

Alberta
Economic Development
6th Floor, Commerce Place
10155–102 Street
Edmonton, Alberta
Canada T5J 4L6
☎ (780) 415-1319
♂ www.alberta-canada.com/aed/mo.cfm

British Columbia
Economic Development
730–999 Canada Place
Vancouver, British Columbia
Canada V6C 3E1
☎ (800) 665-5457
♂ www.gov.bc.ca

Manitoba
Economic Development
The International Business Centre
The Paris Building
1000–259 Portage Avenue
Winnipeg, Manitoba
Canada R3B 3P4
☎ (204) 945-2475
♂ www.gov.mb.ca/iedm/

Newfoundland
Economic Development
10th. Floor, East Block
Confederation Building
St. John's, Newfoundland
Canada A1B 4J6
♂ www.gov.nf.ca/business/

New Brunswick
Economic Development
Centennial Building
PO Box 6000
Fredericton, New Brunswick
Canada E3B 5H1
☎ (506) 444-5228
✆ www.gnb.ca/0398/index-e.asp

Northwest Territories
Economic Development
Government of the
   Northwest Territories
PO Box 1320
Yellowknife, NT
Canada X1A 2L9
✆ www.iti.gov.nt.ca

Nova Scotia
Economic Development
PO Box 2311
14th floor South
Maritime Centre
1505 Barrington Street
Halifax, Nova Scotia
Canada B3J 3C8
☎ (902) 424-0377
✆ www.gov.ns.ca/econ/

Nunavut
Economic Development
Qimugjuk Building 969 on Federal Rd.
PO Box 2200
Iqaluit, Nunavut
Canada X0A 0H0
☎ (867) 975-4500
✆ www.ainc-inac.gc.ca/nu/nuv/
ecd2_e.html

Ontario
Economic Development
8th Floor, Hearst Block
900 Bay St.
Toronto, Ontario
Canada M7A 2E1
☎ (416) 325-6666
✆ www.ontariocanada.com/ontcan/
en/expanding.jsp

Prince Edward Island
Economic Development
94 Euston Street
Charlottetown, PE
Canada C1A 1W4
☎ (902) 368-6300
✆ www.peibusinessdevelopment.com/

Quebec
Economic Development
Tour de la Bourse
800, Victoria Square
Suite 3800, PO Box 247
Montreal, Quebec
Canada H4Z 1E8
☎ (514) 283-6412
✆ www.dec-ced.gc.ca

Saskatchewan
Economic Development
Government of Saskatchewan
919 Saskatchewan Drive
Regina, Saskatchewan
Canada S4P 3V7
☎ (306) 787-2232
✆ www.gov.sk.ca/govt/econdev/

Yukon
Economic Development

Government of Yukon
Box 2703
Whitehorse, Yukon
Canada Y1A 2C6
☎ (867) 393-7014
♂ www.economicdevelopment
.gov.yk.ca/

INDEX